THE STORY OF HAYY IBN YAQZAN
(*risâlat ḫayy ibn yaqzân*)

A Treatise on the Secrets of Oriental Wisdom

by

Abu Bakr Muhammad ibn Tufayl

Translated by
Jim Colville

Dar Ul Thaqafah
https://twitter.com/darulthaqafah
darulthaqafah@gmail.com

2020 CE – 1440 H

THE STORY OF HAYY IBN YAQZAN
by
Abu Bakr Muhammad ibn Tufayl

Translated from the Arabic
with an introduction and notes
by
Jim Colville

CONTENTS

INTRODUCTION

The Story of Hayy ibn Yaqzan (*risâlat ḥayy ibn yaqzân*) is described by its author, Abu Bakr Muhammad ibn Tufayl, as an introduction to the philosophy or "wisdom" intimated by one of the most renowned philosophers of Islam, the Sheikh and Master, Abu 'Ali ibn Sina (Avicenna). It was written to counter what Ibn Tufayl perceived to be the damaging influence of pseudo-philosophic ideas then current in Muslim Spain. *Hayy ibn Yaqzan* is thus, on one level, a sort of primer on mediaeval Islamic philosophy.

The book establishes its frame of reference with a short and selective critique of Islamic philosophy before introducing the narrative framework of a boy of obscure origins reared by a gazelle on a desert island, without human contact. The very uncertainty of the boy's origins is used by the author as an opportunity to include a theory of the origins of life. As the boy gradually becomes aware of his surroundings, he begins to understand that he is somehow different from the other animals, yet superior by virtue of the technical advantages he can realise with his hands.

At the age of seven, the shock of the gazelle's death sets the boy upon the quest which is the book's central theme: the search for the spirit of life. Through sustained observation and reflection, accelerated by the chance discovery of fire and underpinned by his natural intelligence, ingenuity and increasingly more refined reasoning, he acquires mastery of the environment and expertise in the natural sciences.

In parallel with this scientific knowledge, the eponymous Hayy ibn Yaqzan – *i.e.*, "a living son of consciousness" – reasons from the diversity of the world to its wholeness and from the particular objects of sensory perception to an abstract epistemology of universal forms. He infers the existence of God as both the necessary, primary and non-corporeal cause of the universe and its prime mover. Along the way, he deals with many of the major issues of metaphysics. In short, he becomes a philosopher.

His own self, or essence, with which he has perceived the necessarily existent cause of the universe must also, he reasons, be non-corporeal, with the potential to ascend to Him and thereby achieve eternal happiness. He develops a practical plan to achieve this and thus engages with the path to which all knowledge leads and is the purpose of life. Through meditation and exercise, he disciplines himself to transcend sensation and consciousness until finally, at the end of the seventh septenary of his life, he consummates his search.

At this point, he makes the acquaintance of Absal, a doctor of religion and ascetic, who teaches him language and knowledge of the faith (Islam, naturally), which Hayy accepts, although not without some reservation. For his part, Absal recognises that Hayy's wisdom is a transcendent interpretation of revealed religion and a superior achievement to his own profession of faith. Hayy becomes fired with missionary zeal and the two travel to a neighbouring island, where Absal's old friend Salaman is now ruler, on a project to enlighten the population. However, they meet only thinly veiled hostility and, finding even the most likely candidates for enlightenment unable or unwilling to make the necessary commitment, they give up the attempt and return to Hayy's island where they spend the rest of their lives in meditation and devotion.

Within these few pages, the author presents a theory (perhaps testimony is a better word) of human evolution, from apparently random beginnings to purposeful conclusion. Each episode in the story represents a distinct and coherent line of reasoning and is itself a preparation for the next. The result is a systematic treatment of the principal areas of interest to mediaeval Islamic philosophy.

From a modern perspective, it is not difficult to fault *Hayy ibn Yaqzan* on detail. Much of the physics is wrong and there is one unfortunate astronomical error; the anatomy is more theoretical than practical. The author finds some difficulty in maintaining the fiction of Hayy's solitary life. Despite his hero's inability to understand human language, he has him talk to himself on occasion. Moreover, it is not easy to understand how the sophisticated, systematic thinking displayed by Hayy could be accomplished without language. Nevertheless, *Hayy ibn Yaqzan* makes no concession to faith, no provision for saintly intercession and no appeal to the supernatural. The consistency of method makes Hayy's progress apparently relentless but the author never asks his readers to put reason aside or take what he says on trust. Whatever the validity of his inferences for the existence of God, it is hard to suppose, as one commentator has observed, that the subsequent description of the mystic state was imagined merely to provide confirmation.[1] The author acknowledges that there can be no proof:

Introduction

Those who would describe it cannot. Only those who
have united and who know can ever comprehend.

It is the essential seriousness of Ibn Tufayl's rational approach to his
central theme which convinces the reader he is in the company of a refined
and authentic intelligence who is letting him into a secret. *Hayy ibn
Yaqzan* is an exquisitely crafted example of a true philosopher's art.

*

Abu Bakr Muhammad ibn 'Abdulmalik ibn Tufayl – known to the
mediaeval Latin world as Abubacer – was born in the first decade of the
twelfth century in the Andalusian town of Wadi Ash (modern Guadix),
some 60 kilometres north-east of Granada. Little is known of his life. He
studied in Granada, later practising there as a physician until 1154 when he
became secretary to the governor of the province of Ceuta and Tangier. In
1164, he received appointment as court physician at Marrakesh to the
second Almohad Sultan, Abu Ya'qoub Yousuf. The "generous, sincere
and good friend" to whom *Hayy ibn Yaqzan* is formally addressed – while
a wider readership is explicitly sought – is perhaps his patron, the Sultan.

Andalusia[2] in the first half of the twelfth century was beset by a
series of factional conflicts that were temporarily halted by the Almohad[3]
seizure of power, between 1150-70, from a base in Morocco. As well as
bringing a degree of stability to the country and respite from the creeping
gains of the *Reconquista*, the Almohads introduced an ideology inspired by
their founder, Ibn Tumart (died 1130), that called for a return to the
certainty of scriptural sources as the true basis of faith and the rejection of
accretions to worship and belief, sanctioned by custom and time, that the
religious establishment upheld. To this end, the Almohads trained and
appointed politico-religious cadres to positions of legal and administrative
authority throughout their domain. This policy met sustained opposition
from the religious establishment and it is unclear if it ever managed to
secure much popular support – the consensus of historians is that Almohad
authority remained based upon the threat of military force. However, a
conspicuous feature of the Almohad state was the dichotomy between
official, doctrinal orthodoxy and the encouragement of scholarship at court
and, during their seventy-year period of rule, philosophy, science and the
arts prospered within limited circles of privilege.[4]

Ibn Tufayl was proficient in all the sciences of his day and a near-contemporary states having seen writings by him on medicine, physics, philosophy and theology. However, the only extant works which can, with certainty, be attributed to him are *Hayy ibn Yaqzan* and some fragments of verse. It is probable that he wrote *Hayy ibn Yaqzan* sometime between 1169-79.[5] He was responsible for attracting many scholars to the court, including the young Abu'l-Walid Muhammad ibn Rushd (Averroes) who would succeed him as court physician.

As a philosopher, Averroes achieved much wider fame in Latin Europe than Ibn Tufayl but the latter's subsequent influence has been impressive. In 1671, a Latin translation of *Hayy ibn Yaqzan* by Edward Pococke, accompanied by the first printed Arabic text, was published.[6] In 1708, Simon Ockley, professor of Arabic and Cambridge divine, made the first translation from Arabic into English.[7] As a result of Pococke's and Ockley's translations, *Hayy Ibn Yaqzan* attracted much attention throughout Europe in the late seventeenth and early eighteenth centuries and it is likely that the author of that other tale of a desert-island dweller adapted the outline of Ibn Tufayl's book for his own account of a man's achievement of intellectual and spiritual maturity or

> the great work of sincere repentance for my sins, and laying hold of a Saviour for life and salvation, to a stated reformation in practice, and obedience to all God's commands, and this without any teacher or instructor.[8]

Robinson Crusoe was first published in 1719 and, while the logic of the arguments advanced by the prodigal son of the cross might not have impressed the living son of consciousness, many of the reflective passages in Defoe's story are suggestive of Ibn Tufayl's.[9] The influence of *Hayy ibn Yaqzan* has also been identified in the philosophies of Spinosa, Leibnitz and Rousseau.

Ibn Tufayl remained in the Sultan's service until the latter's death in 1184 and survived him by one year, dying in Marrakesh in 1185. By the end of his life, he appears to have abandoned all other interests in favour of prayer and meditation. He was one of the leading and most respected figures of his day and Abu Ya'qoub's son and successor, Mansour, personally led the city in mourning.

*

The historian of science, George Sarton, commended *Hayy ibn Yaqzan* as "one of the most original books of the Middle Ages"[10] yet Ibn Tufayl makes no claim to philosophic originality. Many of the ideas, allegories and proofs he presents are taken from the writings of scholars discussed in the book's introductory section, where the author refers to specific works by Farabi (Alfarabius or Avennasar), Ibn Sina (Avicenna), Ghazzali (Algazel) and Ibn Bajja (Avempace).[11] The influence of Hellenic thought – Aristotelian, Platonic and Neoplatonic – is clearly apparent in *Hayy ibn Yaqzan*.[12] Islamic culture was, of course, the inheritor of the Greek philosophic tradition, much as early Renaissance Europe was to inherit the Islamic tradition.

On certain points, however, philosophy appeared to part company from Islamic doctrine, leading to periodic accusations of unbelief and heresy being raised against philosophers. The apparent contradiction between the Aristotelian doctrine of the sempiternity of the universe – *i.e.*, that is has always been and will always be – and the religious belief in creation in time is a case in point[13] (and one of the most interesting sections in *Hayy ibn Yaqzan* is where Ibn Tufayl has his hero address and reconcile these two beliefs). Although the historical roots of the dispute reach back to the formative stages of Islamic thought, the most coherent attack on metaphysics was made in about 1095 by Abu Hamid Ghazzali, in *The Incoherence of the Philosophers*. Ghazzali later summarised his position in his autobiography, *The Deliverance from Error*:

> It is in theology that most of their [*i.e.*, philosophers'] errors are made and, because the conditions of proof cannot be fulfilled here as they can be in logic, there are numerous disagreements among them. As conveyed by Farabi and Ibn Sina, the teachings of Aristotle sometimes approximate to Islamic doctrines. Their errors are reducible to twenty basic articles, three of which necessitate the charge of unbelief and seventeen the charge of heresy. It was to refute their position on these twenty articles that I wrote *The Incoherence*. The three which contradict the beliefs of all Muslims are: (1) the claim that there is no physical resurrection – *i.e.*, that it is only incorporeal souls which are rewarded or punished

> [in the hereafter] and that reward and punishment are spiritual, not physical; they are quite correct to assert the truth of the spiritual aspect, because it is a fact, but in rejecting the corporeal resurrection they are not only mistaken but have denied scripture; (2) the claim that God has knowledge only of universals and has no knowledge of particulars; this is likewise downright unbelief, the truth being that *neither in the heavens nor on Earth does the weight of a speck of dust escape His attention* [Quran XXXIV, 3]; and (3) the claim that the universe is eternal *a parte ante* and *a parte post*. No Muslim holds any of these beliefs.[14]

In *Hayy ibn Yaqzan*, the relationship between rational metaphysics and revealed religion is represented by the personal meeting between Hayy and Absal and would be dealt with more conventionally by Averroes in his refutation of Ghazzali, *The Incoherence of the Incoherence*. However, the tension between the two is the central, unresolved difficulty for Islamic philosophy, which was never able to free itself completely from a defensive position.

*

The term used by Ibn Tufayl for the philosophy which forms the subject of his book can be read in the Arabic as either *al-ḥikmat al-mashriqîya* ("oriental wisdom") or *al-ḥikmat al-mushriqîya* ("illuminating wisdom"). This has given rise to confusion among some European scholars and led to a supposition that two separate philosophies exist. This is an error.

In the course of a critique of Avicenna's doctrine on the sempiternity of the universe, Averroes says that contemporary followers of Avicenna claim the Master

> called it "oriental philosophy" because it is the doctrine of the Orientals.[15]

He also notes that Avicenna himself believed his approach to be superior to that of the ancient Greek philosophers, from which it may be concluded that, on this issue at least, Avicenna adhered to the doctrine of an eastern system of philosophy that was distinct from the Greek tradition. That this philosophy contains the essential features of what came to be known as *al-ishrâq* or Illuminism – *i.e.,* the second of the two possible readings (in Arabic, *al-ḥikmat al-mushriqîya* is semantically equivalent to *ḥikmat al-ishrâq*) is clear from the substance of *Hayy ibn Yaqzan*. Illuminism is strongly influenced by Sufism[16] and one of its basic tenets is that, while human intellectual development involves rational inquiry, the thinking man eventually needs some sort of metaphysical inspiration, or revelation, to break out of the endless succession of contradictions delivered by scientific knowledge; hence the symbolism of light, which is a feature of this philosophy, and the frequent reference made to the scriptural verse:

> *They will ask you about the spirit. Say, "The spirit proceeds from the command of my Lord, how little is the knowledge that you have been given".*[17]

Critical of the anti-rational approach of some Sufis, Ibn Tufayl presents scientific knowledge and metaphysics as the natural preparation for enlightenment. Whether he intended *Hayy ibn Yaqzan* as an introduction to "oriental wisdom" or "illuminating wisdom" is, therefore, unimportant because the two terms refer here to the same thing.

*

Epistemology is a complicated business in Islamic philosophy, involving an elaborate cosmography (perhaps familiar to readers of Dante) that is central to a proper understanding of *Hayy ibn Yaqzan*. The epistemological theories of Islamic philosophers derive from the Neoplatonic elaboration of an obscure and much discussed Aristotelian theory that conceives of man's potential intellect being actualised by an eternally active intellect, much in the way that light acts upon the faculty of sight:

> Since [just as] in the whole of nature there is something
> which is matter to each kind of thing (and this is what is
> potentially all of them), while on the other hand there is
> something else which is their cause and is productive by
> producing them all – these being related as an art to its
> material – so there must also be these differences in the
> soul. And there is an intellect which is of this kind by

> becoming all things, and there is another which is so by
> producing all things, as a kind of disposition, like light,
> does; for in a way light too makes colours which are
> potential into actual colours. And this intellect is
> distinct, unaffected, and unmixed, being in essence
> activity.[18]

According to the Neoplatonists, two movements operate within the universe – the "emanation" of all things from an original, unitary source that projects itself, without any loss to its own essence, into lower forms of itself, and the subsequent return of all things to that source.[19] The Earth is surrounded by a number of non-material spheres that carry the celestial bodies – *i.e.,* the fixed stars, Saturn, Jupiter, Mars, Venus, Mercury, the Sun and the Moon. These constitute an ordered hierarchy of emanation from the supreme sphere, or zodiac, which governs the entire mechanism. A transcendent "intellect" is associated with each sphere, emanating from the one before and, ultimately, from the one, necessarily existent, primary cause of the universe – *i.e.,* God. In turn, each intellect seeks to return to the original unitary source. The lowest of these intellects, the so-called "active intellect", enlightens the uniquely corruptible, sublunary world in which we live. The individual human intellect may progress through various stages of development, of which the last is to unite with the active intellect, the highest conception of which man is capable and the same for all men. Within this framework, diverse views are held by the *falâsifa* on the role of the active intellect in human knowledge.

According to Ibn Bajja, whose mysticism Ibn Tufayl criticises as theoretical, human perfection is achieved by a process of abstraction from the initial sensory impressions of the material world through a hierarchy of intellectually perceived forms until material knowledge is transcended and the active intellect is reached. This is the final stage of intellectual development, not the result of religious devotion; it is not inconsistent with the account of Hayy ibn Yaqzan's development.

Avicenna, however, held that union with the active intellect is achievable only upon death. In a short treatise of the same name, he had applied the name of Hayy ibn Yaqzan to the active intellect itself. Ibn Tufayl applies the name to an individual, implying that the active intellect is not something external to man and, consequently, that human perfection is something achievable in this life. Ibn Tufayl presents a simplified account of the theory of emanation through the spheres, and does not explicitly refer to the active intellect, but it is clearly there that Hayy witnesses what "no eye has seen, no ear has heard and no heart of man has ever felt".

*

Upon Hayy's meeting with Absal, the book acquires a symbolism where philosophic issues are represented as persons. As the embodiment of the active intellect in man, Hayy is living proof of the perfectibility of human nature through independent, purposeful thought and spiritual discipline. He is the realised being and perfect, self-taught philosopher who has no need of the support of faith. Indeed, it is he who gives Absal, the religious scholar, the key to the interpretation of scripture.

Absal and Salaman represent a long-standing controversy within Islam, frequently with political undertones, between an understanding of scripture based upon esoteric interpretation (*bâṭinîya*) as distinct from its acceptance as literal truth (*zâhirîya*). This issue is explored in detail and in a more conventionally philosophic way by Averroes in *The Definitive Statement*. The meeting between Hayy and Absal represents the underlying accord between philosophy and enlightened religious belief, although the moral is nevertheless clear that what a man achieves for himself is more satisfying than what he inherits from convention. Salaman and the little band of hopefuls whom Hayy endeavours to enlighten represent the guardians of established, traditional faith and concomitant moral fabric of society, while the mass of the population are, alas, no better than cattle. With Hayy's failure to enlighten Salaman, the book ends on a pessimistic note. True knowledge which, in their different ways, both wisdom and faith point towards, is a privilege reserved for the very few.

The author of *Hayy ibn Yaqzan* navigates by a compass whose needle points to heaven. If, at times, the book's brevity and choice of narrative format leave the reader's questions unanswered (for example, over the role of conscience) Ibn Tufayl claims to offer no more than a brief glimpse of "the secrets behind the veil" that true wisdom offers, as *a sign for the man with a heart, with ears to hear and eyes with which to see*.[20]

***

NOTES

[1] *Encyclopaedia of Islam*[2], Vol. III (Leiden, E.J. Brill: 1971), *s.v. Hayy b. Yakzân* (A.-M. Goichon).

[2] Given the variable balance of power during the twelfth century, it is difficult to define accurately the area of Spain and Portugal under Muslim control. Loosely, however, the name Andalusia can be applied at this time to an area covering slightly more than the southern third of the Iberian peninsula – *i.e.*, the area south of a line drawn roughly between Lisbon and Valencia, with a dip around Toledo.

[3] In Arabic, *al-muwahhidûn* (Almohad) means 'Unitarians'.

[4] For an account of the historical background, see H. Kennedy, *Muslim Spain and Portugal* (London, Longman: 1996), p. 196 ff.

[5] L. Gauthier, *Ibn Thofail – sa vie, ses oeuvres* (Paris: 1909), p. 43.

[6] E. Pococke (trans.), *Philosophus Autodidactus, sive epistola de Hai ebn Yokdhan* (Oxford: 1671).

[7] S. Ockley (trans.), *The Improvement of Human Reason Exhibited in the Life of Hai ebn Yoqdhan* (London: 1708).

[8] D. Defoe, *Robinson Crusoe*, ed. A. Ross (London, Penguin: 1965), p. 222-223.

[9] For a detailed comparison of the two, see A. Pastor, *The Idea of Robinson Crusoe* (Watford: 1930). At the time of writing, I was unaware of *The World of Ibn Tufayl: Interdisciplinary Perspectives on Hayy ibn Yaqdhan*, ed. L. I. Conrad (Leiden, E.J. Brill: 1996).

[10] G. Sarton, *Introduction to the History of Science* (Washington: 1931), Vol. 2, p. 354.

[11] See Notes to the translation for brief biographical details.

[12] Background influences from Greek philosophy are identified in detail in L. E. Goodman, *Ibn Tufayl's Hayy ibn Yaqzan* (New York, Tayne: 1972), pp. 176 ff.; the channels of transmission are less clear.

[13] In modern terms, these might be reworded as 'steady state' and 'big bang' theories, respectively.

[14] A. Marraq (ed.), *al-munqidh min al-dalâl lil-ghazzâli* (Tunis: 1989), p. 55 ff.

[15] M. Bouyges (ed.), *Averroes, tahâfut al-tahâfut* (Beirut: 1930), p. 421; English translation by S. van den Bergh, *Averroes' Tahafut al-Tahafut*, 2 Vols. (London, Luzac: 1954).

[16] For an introduction to Sufism, see I. Shah, *The Sufis* (New York, Doubleday: 1964).

[17] Quran XVII, 85; see *Encyclopaedia of Islam*[2], Vol. IV, *s.v. Ishrâk* (R. Arnaldez).

[18]Aristotle, *De Anima, Books II & III*, trans. D. W. Hamlyn (Oxford, Clarendon Press: 1993), p. 60 — Bk. III, Ch. 5 (430^a10).
[19]See *The Oxford Companion to Philosophy*, ed. T. Honderich (Oxford University Press: 1995), *s.v. Neoplatonism.*
[20]Quran L, 37.

THE STORY OF HAYY IBN YAQZAN
(*risâlat ḥayy ibn yaqzân*)

A Treatise on the Secrets of Oriental Wisdom

by

Abu Bakr Muhammad ibn Tufayl

My generous, sincere and good friend, may God grant you joy and life everlasting! You asked me to tell you what I can of the secrets of oriental wisdom that the Master and Imam, Sheikh Abu 'Ali ibn Sina spoke of.[1] You should be aware at the outset that whoever wishes to know the clear, transparent truth must devote himself completely to its pursuit and consummation.

Your request was itself the sublime inspiration which led me (may God be praised) to bear witness to a state that I had not experienced before, a destination too strange and mysterious for words to describe or explain, as it belongs to a domain and world of which words have no part. Yet the rapture, bliss and delight of that state are such that the man who finally arrives upon its frontiers cannot conceal its quality or hide its secret. In fact, the energy, the ecstasy and the joy he feels compel him to reveal it, although in broad outline rather than in detail. Those whose mastery of the sciences is less than complete have, however, spoken of it rashly and comments such as, "Praise be to my own glorious self!",[2] "I am the One Truth!"[3] and "It is God within the clothes I wear!" have been made. Sheikh Abu Hamid Ghazzali (may God bless him) represented his own attainment of this state with the following line of verse:

> It was what it was but to tell there's no way,
> So think only good and don't ask me to say.[4]

But he, of course, was a well-educated man with a mind disciplined by learning.

Let us consider what Abu Bakr ibn Sa'igh[5] said when discussing the quality of conjunction with the Intellect:

> When the concept has been understood, it will become
> clear that it cannot possibly be known or conceived of at
> the level of the conventional sciences but rather at a level

where one realises oneself dissociated from everything before and where other, non-material relationships apply. This level is too sublime to be attached to the physical world and is quite independent of its structure. It is a set of states of bliss that could be described as divine states, given by God to those of his slaves as He wills.[6]

This level to which Abu Bakr refers is attained by the methods of theoretical metaphysics and rational speculation; there is no doubt that he himself attained it, even if he did not pass beyond. However, the level of which we speak is something else, not in the sense that there is anything different to be discovered but in respect of a greater clarity and the witness to what might be called "power" only metaphorically, since neither ordinary language nor specialised terminology contain the words to refer to the thing to which this kind of vision bears witness. This state of which I speak, and which your request moved me to experience directly, is one of those noted by the Master, Abu 'Ali:

> By will and discipline, he [the mystic] reached a point where ecstatic glimpses of the light of truth sparkled then faded, like flashes of lightning. As he maintained his discipline, these overwhelming states became more frequent and by sustaining it, he achieved rapture without effort. Whatever he looked at would point him towards paradise. He speaks of being overwhelmed by a state in which saw reality in almost everything. Further discipline brought him to a point where time is turned into perfect stillness,[7] where what was once fleeting becomes constant and what had been a faint glimmer becomes a bright shooting-star. And there comes to him a sure, certain knowledge, like a lasting friendship.

He described a hierarchy of levels of which the last is where

> his deepest being becomes like a flawless mirror facing the truth. Waves of sublime ecstasy wash over him and to see the image of the truth is the rapture of his soul. At this level, he sees the truth and he sees his own soul – as it is seeing – and looks from one to the other. He then

loses all consciousness of himself, seeing only paradise, and there achieves union.[8]

In describing these states, it was only Sheikh Abu 'Ali's intention to give an impression, not a reasoned inference from premise to conclusion. If you would like an illustration of how differently from others such people perceive, imagine a man who is naturally intelligent with sound intuition, a good memory and a sharp mind but who has been blind from birth. This man has grown up in the city and, by means of his other senses, has come to recognise people and many of the various animals, objects, streets, alleys, houses and shops to the point where he can find his way around without a guide. He recognises everyone he meets right away. He is aware of colours only by name and by certain denotations. Now, at some point, his eyes are opened and he gains the power of sight. As he walks around the city, he finds nothing to contradict his preconceptions and even colours appear to coincide with the mental picture he had of them. However, there are two important and related differences – an increased clarity and an enormous pleasure and delight.

The condition of the philosopher who has not attained the state of holiness is like the initial condition of the blind man. The things described by Abu Bakr as too sublime to be attached to the physical world and given by God to those of His slaves as He wills, are like the colours known only to him by name and denotation. But the condition of the philosopher who has attained that state and to whom God has granted that thing which we have metaphorically called power, is like the blind man who has gained the power of sight.

It is exceptional to find a philosopher who is so clear-sighted that he has no need of speculation. By "speculation", I mean neither the materialist knowledge of philosophers nor the transcendent knowledge of the holy; these two kinds of knowledge are totally different and must not be confused. What I mean by "speculation" is the rational metaphysics practised by the likes of Abu Bakr.

It is, however, implicit in metaphysics that it be valid and true and, in this respect, a parallel emerges between Abu Bakr's position and the perception of the holy. The latter speak of precisely the same things but with greater clarity and a rapture quite sublime. Abu Bakr criticised the way that Sufis talk about this rapture. He said it has to do with the power of imagination and promised to give a clear description of the consequent state. You know, he really should be told: "Do not say something's sweet if you've never tasted it or pick a quarrel with two friends at once!" Anyway, he never kept his promise. Perhaps, as he claimed, it was lack of time and his preparation for the move to Oran that prevented him. Or maybe he thought that by describing this state, he would have been obliged to say things that compromised his own lifestyle and contradicted his promotion of money-making schemes! However, I have digressed – albeit necessarily – from my response to your request.

It would appear that you have one of two reasons for making the request. On the one hand, you may wish to know what it is that those who bear witness, experience the truth and enter into the presence see in their state of holiness. It is impossible to state this reality in words. When one tries to press language into service, the reality changes and turns into something speculative. A man's testimony alters beyond recognition when he tries to close in on that world with language. Ways of describing it differ enormously, words slip out of control and men stray from the straight path without realising that it is they, not others, who are lost. The truth, you see, is something infinite, with a multitude of aspects that encompass but are not themselves encompassed.

On the other hand, you may wish me to introduce you to this subject through the methods of systematic reasoning. Now that (and may God bless you with closeness unto Him) is something which it is possible to speak of and to put down in writing but it is rarer than the philosopher's stone, especially in this land of ours. Curiously, only a very few individuals have managed to convey anything at all about it and, even then, only symbolically. The Islamic establishment has given explicit warning and forbidden any involvement.

You should certainly not assume that the extant philosophical writings of Aristotle and Farabi, or Ibn Sina's *The Healing*,[9] are sufficient by themselves, or that any Andalusian has written about it in a satisfactory manner. Before logic and metaphysics developed here, scholars occupied themselves exclusively with mathematics, in which they reached an advanced level but failed to take matters further. Their successors made some progress in logic and demonstrated an intellectual curiosity in our subject but, nonetheless, were not led to perfect truth. One of them wrote these lines:

> The sciences of men are of only two kinds
> And anything more is impossible to find:
> A true, which to try and obtain is futility
> And a false which, when mastered, has no utility.[10]

They, in turn, were followed by more sophisticated thinkers who came closer to the truth. Among these, Abu Bakr ibn Sa'igh had the subtlest mind, the soundest reasoning and the most genuine perception. However, he was preoccupied with mundane matters and died before the hidden treasures of his wisdom could be disseminated. Most of his extant works, for example, *On the Soul* and *The Organisation of the Solitary Life*, as well as his writings on logic and physics, are incomplete. Those which are complete are merely summaries, as he himself acknowledges. He admits that he was able to give expression to his theme in *The Treatise on the Conjunction of the Intellect with Man* only with difficulty and after much effort. His style leaves something to be desired, in places and, had time permitted, he might have been inclined to revise.

This, then, is what is known to me of Ibn Sa'igh's state of learning. I did not meet him personally and have never read anything by those of his contemporaries who are said to be his equals. Thereafter, we come to our own contemporaries – who are either still at the formative stage,[11] have no interest in perfection, or are unknown to me.

Most of the extant works of Abu Nasr Farabi[12] deal with logic; those dealing with metaphysics are highly sceptical. In *The Principled Beliefs of the Superior Community*,[13] he asserts the existence, after death, of evil souls in eternal torment. Then, in *Politics*, he claims they will be obliterated and end up in nothingness, with only consummate and superior souls being eternal. In his commentary on Aristotle's *Ethics*, he describes human happiness as something existing only on the plane of this earthly life. He goes on to say what could be paraphrased to the effect that everything else is irrational and the superstition of old women. This deprives mankind of any hope of the Mercy of God and places good and evil on the same level by making nothingness the fate of all. He slips up here and his position does not thereafter recover. Additionally, he maligns prophecy claiming that it is only a particular kind of imaginative power and expresses his preference for philosophy. He expresses other views that there is no need to discuss here.

Sheikh Abu 'Ali was a commentator of Aristotle and follower of his school of thought. He wrote *The Healing* within the framework of the Peripatetic system.   Nevertheless, he claims at the beginning of that book that the truth, in his view, lies elsewhere and refers us to his *Oriental Philosophy*.   The reader of *The Healing* and the Aristotelian corpus will observe that, in most cases, they are consistent, although the former discusses several topics on which we are unaware of Aristotle's views. If both are considered literally, without discerning their deeper, esoteric meaning, the reader will not attain to any sort of perfection, as Sheikh Abu 'Ali himself indicates in *The Healing*.

The writings of Sheikh Abu Hamid Ghazzali,[14] addressed as they are to a popular audience, contain inconsistencies; he levels the charge of unbelief against things that he himself later accepts. For example, in *The Incoherence of the Philosophers*, he criticises philosophers for, among other things, rejecting the physical resurrection of the body and asserting reward or punishment only for souls. At the beginning of *The Balance of Action*,[15] he claims that these beliefs are held by all leading Sufis, without exception.   Then, in *The Deliverance from Error and Explanation of the States*,[16] he states that he himself holds Sufi beliefs, although reaching this position only after prolonged study.

His writings contain many examples of this sort, as anyone who studies them carefully will discover. He defends his position at the end of *The Balance of Action* where he describes three categories of beliefs: those commonly held by the masses, those addressed in response to a question or request for guidance and those held privately and only expressed to others holding similar beliefs. He goes on to say,

> If the result of this is to cause doubt in traditional beliefs
> then that will be benefit enough. Without doubt there is
> no critical examination and without critical examination
> there is no perception. The man who does not perceive
> remains in blindness and confusion.

He expressed this idea with the following verse:

> Leave aside what you have heard,
> Accept what you see with your eyes,

Saturn's faint glimmer shines dimly beside
The radiant morning sunrise.

This is characteristic of Sheikh Abu Hamid's teaching – largely symbolic and obscurantist, of use principally to someone who had first studied his writings carefully and then listened to his personal commentary, or to someone approaching his work with an open and discerning mind and for whom the simplest of allusions is enough.

He states in his *Book of Gems* that he has written other works, withheld from general circulation, that contain unambiguous explanations of the truth. As far as I am aware, none of these has reached Andalusia. Some of his writings that are available, including *Intellectual Knowledge*, *The Rising and the Levelling* and *Miscellaneous Questions*, have been claimed, mistakenly, as these esoteric works but while they do contain certain allusions, they provide little more insight than we find in his well-known works. *The Sublime Destination* seems to contain something more enigmatic but he himself has stated that it does not belong among his esoteric writings, which implies that neither do any of the above.

A recent critic has supposed from the conclusion to *The Tabernacle of Lights* that Sheikh Abu Hamid committed a grave error and fell into an abyss from which there is no escape when, having discussed the categories of those veiled by light, he carries on to say that those who attain holiness ascribe to the Supreme Being an attribute incompatible with His absolute oneness.[17] This critic holds it then follows that Sheikh Abu Hamid himself believes the Divine Essence admits of multiplicity. How far exalted is God above the claims of these dark minds!

In my opinion, there is no doubt that Sheikh Abu Hamid is one of those who have arrived at the sublime and holy destination and achieved ultimate rapture. However, his esoteric writings which seek to comprehend direct illumination have not reached us.

*

I have not arrived independently at the truth I have experienced. I have carefully studied the teachings of Sheikh Abu Hamid and Sheikh Abu 'Ali, relating one to the other, and compared them with contemporary ideas fashionable among so-called philosophers. It was thus through study and systematic reasoning that I established the existence of the truth and only subsequently have I had a slight taste of it by direct experience. Now I believe that I myself am in a position to influence by my teaching and you, with your self-evident sincerity and honesty in making the request, are the first to receive what knowledge I have to impart.

However, simply lecturing on the furthest limits of my own experience before establishing first principles would be of no more use to you than a conventional summary. I say this in the spirit of goodwill and friendship and because I know you respect me, not because I think that what I have to say should be accepted without question. It is not my intention to content you with the rudiments; I want something much higher for you. They are not enough for salvation, let alone to scale the heights.

I wish to lead you along the paths that I have followed and let you swim in the sea that I have crossed so that you might reach the same destination. Then you may bear witness to what I have witnessed, realise through the perception of your soul what I have realised and liberate your understanding from the constraint of my teaching. This will require no small amount of time, freedom from distraction and a willingness to devote yourself fully to the task. But if you are sincere in your intention and genuine in your resolve to set out upon the quest then, when the morning light has broken, you will indeed be grateful for your journey[18] and find your labour well rewarded. You will have pleased your Lord and He will have contented you.

For myself, I will be at your disposal whenever you require and hope that I can lead you along the path that is the straightest and the safest from dangers and pitfalls.

Now, to give a brief glimpse to encourage you to set out upon the path, I will tell the story of Hayy ibn Yaqzan, Absal[19] and Salaman, as Sheikh Abu 'Ali named them. Their story contains a lesson for those who can understand and *a sign for the man who has a heart, has ears to hear and eyes with which to see.*[20]

∗∗∗

Our pious forebears (may God be pleased with them) told the story of an island lying off the coast of India, on the equator, where a human being was born without mother and father. This island enjoys the most temperate climate on Earth and is perfectly receptive to the highest sunlight – although most conventional philosophers and natural scientists

10

disagree with this view, maintaining that the most temperate area on Earth is the fourth region.[21]

{If they argued that the absence of centres of population on the equator is a function of unfavourable geographical factors, their claim might not be unreasonable. But when they argue, as most of them do, that it is a function of extremely high temperatures, it can be demonstrated that they are mistaken.

In physics, it has been proven that heat can be caused in one of three ways: by motion, conduction or light. It has also been established that the sun is neither essentially hot, nor is it involved in any sort of inter-action. Smooth, non-transparent bodies are the most receptive to light. Coarse, opaque bodies are partially receptive, while transparent bodies with no trace of opacity are completely unreceptive to light. Sheikh Abu 'Ali was the first to demonstrate this, among other things. If these premisses are held to be sound, it follows that the sun does not heat the earth by conduction since, in essence, the sun is not hot. Nor is the earth heated by motion, since it is stationary – in the same position at sunset as at sunrise (although there are perceptible temperature differences at these times). Nor does the sun first heat the atmosphere, which subsequently heats the earth. How could that be so when, during warm weather, we discover the lower atmosphere to be much hotter than the upper?

We are, therefore, left with the conclusion that the sun heats the earth by means of light alone. Heat always follows light, which is why light focused in a concave mirror will set on fire whatever it is directed at.

Definitive mathematical proofs have established that both the earth and the sun are spherical in shape, with the latter being much larger. The area of the earth in sunlight at any given time is always greater than one-half and the sunlight is at its most intense in the middle of this area because it faces a greater surface of the sun and is furthest from the peripheral darkness. The closer to the earth's periphery, the less sunlight there is until, beyond the periphery, there is total and permanent darkness.

In the central region, the temperature is hottest when the sun is at the zenith, particularly so the longer it remains there. In places where the sun is furthest off the zenith, the temperature is extremely cold. However, it has been established in astronomy that the sun is at the zenith over the equator only twice a year – once when it enters the constellation of Aries and again when it enters the constellation of Libra. For the rest of year, the sun is over the northern and southern hemispheres for six months each. Temperatures at the equator are, therefore, neither excessively hot nor excessively cold and, consequently, the climate there is moderate.

These matters require further explanation and constitute something of a digression from our theme. I have drawn attention to them only because they have been adduced in support of the possibility of the spontaneous creation, in this region, of a human being without mother and father.}

According to one version of the story, Hayy ibn Yaqzan was one of a number of individuals created there without mother or father but that account has been challenged. The alternative version[22] goes as follows:

A neighbouring island, rich and prosperous with a large population and abundant resources, was ruled by a proud and jealous king. This king had a sister of great beauty whom he kept in seclusion and would not allow to marry, having found no proper match for her. However, she formed a clandestine relationship with a man called Yaqzan and they married in secret, although in conformity with the conventions of the time. She conceived and gave birth to a little boy but was terrified of the scandal that would follow if her secret should ever become known. So, after feeding him, she placed the child inside a chest[23] and secured the lid. At nightfall, she went with her servants and closest friends to the seashore where, her heart aflame with anxiety and grief, she bade farewell to him:

"Lord, You created this child whose existence has never been spoken of. I carried and nourished him within me until his body was formed. Now I surrender him to Your grace and mercy, for fear of what that cruel and heartless tyrant will do. Most merciful God, be with him always and protect him." Then she threw the chest into the swell.

During the night, the force of the waves and the tide carried the chest to the neighbouring island, mentioned above. At that time of year, the tide reaches its highest level and the chest was washed into a lush, mangrove swamp where it was sheltered from the wind and rain and shaded from the sun – *whose rays shone obliquely when it rose and when it set*. As the tide ebbed, the chest was left stranded. The wind blew the sand into dunes, filling the inlet and cutting the chest off from the sea.

As he grew hungry and restless, the infant began to cry for attention. He was heard by a gazelle whose foal had been carried off by an eagle and, thinking it was the crying of her foal, she followed the noise to the chest.   Hearing the cries coming from inside, she kicked it with her hooves until a top panel broke off (the force of the waves had already loosened the nails that held the panels). Immediately, she felt a maternal love for the infant and gave him the milk of her breast to drink. The gazelle remained close by thereafter, looked after him and kept him safe from harm.

This is how the story begins according to those who reject the idea of spontaneous creation. Later, we will describe how the boy grew up and passed through the stages of development before achieving sublime fulfilment.

*

The version which claims that he was born from the earth describes how, beneath the island, deep within the earth, there was a great mass of clay that had been in a state of ferment over the course of many years.   Hot vapours mixed with cold and moist vapours fused with dry to produce a homogenous balance of forces. In some parts, the mixture of vapours developed a greater balance and disposition to form humours[24] than in others.   The most perfect balance was in the centre, where the vapours most fully resembled the humours of man.

As the clay churned, bubbles were formed by its extreme viscosity.   In the centre, a tiny bubble formed that split into two, separated by a fine membrane and each part filled with a gentle, ethereal substance of the most suitable balance.   At that point, the spirit that proceeds from the command of the Lord attached itself and so firmly did it bind, it would have been hard for either sense or reason to separate the two. This spirit emanates eternally from God – His are the power and the glory – and could be likened to the sunlight shining constantly on Earth.

{Now, air is a highly transparent body and is thus not illuminated by sunlight. Coarse, unpolished bodies are partially illuminated but differ in respect of their receptivity to light, so their colours differ accordingly. Smooth, polished objects, such as mirrors and the like, are fully illumi-nated.   The concentration of light in a specially-shaped, concave mirror, causes fire.   In a similar way does the spirit from God radiate upon all existing things.   However, there are some things in which no trace of the spirit appears due to their lack of receptivity. These are inanimate, lifeless objects and could be likened to the air in the above example. Some trace of the spirit appears in plants by virtue of their disposition and they, in turn, might be likened to coarse, opaque objects. And there are some existing things in which its trace is very visible. These are the species of animal life, which are equivalent to the smooth, polished objects in the our example.

Just as certain smooth objects are highly receptive to sunlight and resemble the form and image of the sun, so certain animals are extremely receptive to the spirit, being formed in its image and bearing a resemblance to it. Such is mankind and is what the Prophet referred to with the words, "God created Adam in His image."

If this image becomes so strong within a man that all other forms vanish within it and it alone remains, the radiance of its light burns everything it touches. Its likeness is then that of the concave mirror reflecting upon itself and setting fire to whatever its light is directed at. This is the case only with the prophets (may God bless them) and has been properly explained elsewhere. Let us now complete the account of spontaneous creation.}

When the spirit attached itself to the chamber, the account continues, all faculties became subject to it, made absolutely obedient by the Will of God. Alongside this chamber, another bubble formed that divided into three, each part separated from the others by delicate membranes but connected by pathways and filled with an ethereal substance similar to that which filled the first, only more delicate. In these three hollow spaces divided from one, a set of subject faculties was located, charged with the protection and preservation of their hosts and the transmission of any impression, however subtle, to the primary spirit attached to the first chamber.

Beside these two chambers, a third bubble formed, filled with an ethereal substance similar to, but coarser than, the first two. A set of subject faculties was located there and likewise charged with its protection and preservation. These three chambers were the first to be created from the great fermenting mass of clay, in the manner we have outlined.[25]

Each had need of the others. The first needed the service and utility of the other two, while they needed the first, as the governed need a governor and the led require a leader. To subsequently created organs, however, the latter two stood in the relation of governor to governed, with the second being more suited to this than the third.

When the spirit attached to the first chamber, its temperature rose and it took on a conical, flame-like shape. The coarse substance surrounding it took on a similar shape and became solid tissue, around which a protective membrane formed. This entire organ is known as the heart. Because of the exhaustion of vapours following its temperature rise, the heart could not have long survived without something to supply nutrition and compensate for its continuous action. It also required the ability to sense what it may be in harmony and conflict with, in order to attract and repel accordingly. By virtue of their faculties, whose source is the heart itself, the other two organs supplied these needs – the brain providing feeling and the liver supplying nutrition. In turn, the brain and liver required the heart to supply them with heat and their specific faculties, of which it is the source. As a result, a network of connections and pathways developed, some wider than others, as dictated by necessity. These are the arteries and veins.

This version of the story goes on to describe the process of formation and development of the organs in great detail, in the same way that natural scientists describe the development of the embryo in the womb until, with development complete and all the organs formed, the foetus is ready to descend.

To conclude the description, we are again referred to the great mass of fermenting clay and how its condition was such as to furnish everything required for human creation, including the membranes surrounding the foetus. When development was complete, the membranes split – as in normal labour – and what was left of the clay dried up and cracked. With its source of nutrition gone, the infant became hungry and cried for attention. It was then that the bereaved gazelle came to the rescue and from this point on, the two versions of the story coincide.

*

His adoptive mother lived in a fertile land of plenty and her rich, abundant milk provided excellent nourishment. She remained close by at all times, leaving him alone only when it was absolutely necessary to find food. He became so attached to the gazelle that, if she stayed away too long, his screaming grew louder and louder until she came running back.

In the absence of predatory beasts on the island, the child grew up in safety, raised and nourished on the gazelle's milk until two years had passed, and he began to walk and grow teeth. He followed the gazelle everywhere and she stayed close by to look after him. She took him to places where fruit trees grew and fed him the sweet, ripe fruits that had fallen. Any with hard shells she cracked open with her teeth. When he wanted milk, she suckled him and when thirsty, she took him to water. If he was hot, she shaded him and when cold, she warmed him. Each night, she took him back to where she had found him and lay down beside him, sheltering him with her own body and the feathers which had filled the chest when he had first been laid inside.[26] They lived among a herd of gazelles that roamed, pastured and slept together.

The child began to imitate the gazelle's voice, until it was scarcely possible to tell the two apart. As need arose, he also learned to imitate birdsong and the sounds of other animals accurately. Mostly, however, it was the sounds of the gazelles he imitated, whether to call out for help or in friendship, to invite or to threaten (since, in different circumstances, animals make different sounds). The wild animals were as accustomed to him as he was to them; they did not reject him nor did he reject them and, as experiences impressed themselves upon his mind, he formed a liking for some and a dislike of others.

However, he could not help noticing that all the animals were covered with fur or hair or feathers He saw how fast they could run, how strong they were and how they had natural weapons, like antlers, horns, fangs, hooves and talons with which to defend themselves. By comparison, he was naked and unarmed, slow and weak. Any animal that challenged him for fruit invariably overpowered him and took everything for itself. He could neither defend himself against or outrun any. The young gazelles with whom he had grown up began to grow antlers where none had been before and to develop speed where before they had been slow. He saw none of these developments in himself and think as he might, could find no explanation. He studied the disabled and handicapped animals but did not believe himself to be like them.

Likewise, he noticed that the animals' waste orifices were covered, by a tail in the case of the orifice of coarse waste and hair, or the like, in the case of the other. Their penises were also less visible than his, which unsettled and disturbed him. He was now almost seven and had been brooding on these matters for some time. Distressed by his shortcomings and despairing of any change, he picked several broad leaves and, with some in front and some behind, fastened them around his waist with a sort of belt made from esparto grass and palm fibre. But, in no time, the leaves dried out and fell off. He persisted nevertheless, collecting more and pleating them together. These lasted, perhaps, a little longer but, at any rate, not for very long. He cut and trimmed a branch and used it to chase away any animals who threatened him. He thus found he could now get the better of the weaker ones and at least put up a good fight against the stronger. This gave him some sense of self-respect.

He came to realise that his hands gave him many advantages over the beasts. He could cover his nakedness with leaves and defend what was his with sticks. These compensated for his lack of a tail and natural defences. And so he grew up to reach the age of seven, although renewing the leaves to cover himself was a constant nuisance.

The idea then occurred to him of removing the tail of a dead animal and attaching it to himself as a covering but he noticed how anxious the animals were to avoid their dead and this made him feel uneasy about acting. One day, however, he came across the body of a dead eagle that the animals did not seem to be avoiding and seized his opportunity. He first cut off the wings and tail feathers, keeping them intact and fanning out the feathers. He then removed the remains of the skin and cut it into two, tying one piece to his back and covering his belly, and below, with the other. He hung the tail feathers over his buttocks and covered his shoulders with the wings. This not only gave protection and warmth but also earned him the respect of the wild animals who now no longer challenged or threatened him.

In fact, only the gazelle who had nursed him and raised him ever came near. The two never strayed far apart, until she grew too old and weak to fend for herself and it was now his turn to lead her to the fertile lands and gather ripe fruits for her.

The gazelle grew thinner and weaker, until at last death caught up with her and all her movements and responses ceased. Seeing her like that, the boy was overwhelmed with sadness and his soul could almost have burst in grief. He called to her in the same voice that she used to answer him, and as loudly as he could, but she made not the slightest response.

He looked into her eyes and ears and examined her limbs, trying to find the source of the disorder and remove it in the hope that she would recover but he saw no obvious sign of anything wrong. This idea was inspired by having already noticed in himself that, when he closed his eyes or covered them with something, he was unable to see until he took away the cover. When he put his fingers in his ears, he could not hear until he took them out and if he held his nose, he would smell nothing until he let go. Movement and the senses, he concluded, could be inhibited but would return to normal when the impediments were removed. However, he saw no obvious sign on the gazelle's body of anything wrong and, at the same time, her inactivity was total and not confined to any one limb.

It then occurred to him that the malady from which she suffered was, perhaps, hidden from sight in one of her internal organs. That organ, he reckoned, must be indispensable to the functioning of the external limbs and when it had become sick, the disorder had spread and the paralysis became general. If he could find this organ and remove whatever had affected it, the resulting benefit would, he believed, spread throughout her whole body and she would recover the power of movement.

He had previously observed in the bodies of dead animals that only the skull, chest and belly had cavities and this led him to think that the organ he was looking for must lie in one of these three places. He became convinced that it had to be the middle one, since he was sure that every other limb and organ must be dependent upon it. Moreover, when he considered himself, he felt that this sort of organ had to be in the chest. He could imagine himself doing without the rest of his limbs and organs – hands, arms, ears, nose or eyes and even his head, he suspected, was not absolutely essential[27] – but it seemed impossible to do without the thing inside his chest. He noticed that, any time he fought an animal, he would instinctively protect his chest from its horns, because of a feeling that there was something special inside.

Concluding that the sick organ had to be inside the gazelle's chest, he decided to locate and examine it, to perhaps discover the disorder and remove it. What held him back was a fear that doing so might cause more damage than the malady itself and only make her worse. But he realised that he had never seen any animal that had been in this condition and recovered. She had no hope of recovery if he left her as she was while there was, at least, some hope if he could find the organ and remove the disorder. So he made up his mind to cut open her breast and examine inside.

Using sharp pieces of stone and dry splinters of cane in place of knives, he pierced her chest, cutting through the ribcage and arriving at the diaphragm.[28] Its very toughness made him think it must be protecting a vital organ and that, if he cut through, he would find what he was looking for. A lack of instruments other than stones or cane made this difficult but he sharpened them and began working again, carefully, until he eventually cut through to the lung. At first he thought this was the organ he was looking for and he studied it, trying to find the disorder.

However, he had uncovered only one half of the lung and it lay off-centre, while he believed that the organ he was looking for would be in the very centre of the body, in terms of length and breadth. So he carried on probing the middle of the chest, until he came to the heart. It was surrounded by extremely solid tissue and partially covered by the lung on the side where he had made the first incision.

"If this organ looks the same from the other side," he thought, "it must lie in the very centre and so will be the one I am looking for. It seems to be in the right place and to have the correct shape. It's solid and compact and is covered by tissue in a way that none of the other organs are."

When he examined the other side of the chest, he discovered the diaphragm and the lung in the same positions and concluded that the heart was indeed the organ he was looking for. He worked hard to remove the tissue and cut through the heart strings which, after wearing himself out with the effort, he succeeded in doing.

He exposed the heart and observed the uniformity of its shape but found no apparent mark of disorder. However, when he squeezed it, it appeared to be hollow.

"Perhaps what I am really looking for is inside and still remains to be discovered."

So he cut open the heart and found the two ventricles, the right one filled with congealed blood and the left one empty.

"What I'm looking for has to be in one of these two chambers but on the right there is only blood that must have congealed after the body arrived at this state," he thought, having already noticed how blood clots after flowing from a wound. "It's just ordinary blood which is found in every organ and is not specific to one.   What I've been looking for all along has to be something unique and indispensable and this just doesn't fit the description.   After all, how many times have I been wounded by animals and lost lots of blood but it hasn't incapacitated me or stopped me from moving?   This chamber, then, does not have what I'm looking for. And the left-hand one is empty, so does that mean that it's obsolete? Every organ has a specific function so how can this one, given its importance, be useless?   I'm certain that what I've been looking for was once here but has since vanished, leaving the chamber empty like this. Consequently, the whole body suffered paralysis, lost consciousness and became incapable of movement."

Concluding that whatever had once occupied the chamber had disappeared before he had even started cutting, he realised that it would be unlikely to return after all the damage done since. He began to think of the body as something of little worth, with no value over and above that thing which, he believed, occupies it for a time and then departs.

He focused his thoughts upon that thing. What is it? What does it look like?   How does it attach to the body?   Where did it go? How did it exit the body?   What made it leave, if it was forced to leave?   And if it left from   choice, what made the body so repellent to make it want to go?

His mind was so full of these questions that he gave no more thought to the physical body in front of him. He knew only that it was the mother who had raised and cared for him that had gone. It was from her that those actions had emanated, not this useless body. The entire body was just an instrument for those actions, much like the stick hc himself used to fight the wild animals. His thoughts turned away from the physi-cal body towards what had possessed and animated it and for that alone he longed.

Meanwhile, the corpse had begun to decay and give off a foul smell. This increased his aversion to it and he would have preferred not to look at it at all.   Then he noticed two ravens fighting and one strike the other dead. The survivor began scraping a hole in the ground into which it placed its victim.

"It was wrong of the raven to kill the other," thought the boy, "but it has done the right thing by burying the corpse and has shown me what I ought to do with my mother's body."[29]

So he dug a hole, laid his mother's body inside and covered it with earth.

He continued to speculate about the thing that activates the body but had no idea what it might be. Looking at the other gazelles and how they had the same shape and form as his mother, he became convinced that each was animated and activated by something similar to the thing that had animated and activated his mother. Because of this, he felt a bond with them and stayed close.

For a time, this was how he remained. Walking alone around the shore, he kept watch for anything that resembled him, in the way that every single animal and plant had many others that resembled it. But he found nothing. He surveyed his island surrounded by sea on all sides and believed that there was nowhere else in existence.

*

It happened that, one day, friction in the undergrowth caused a brush fire to break out. When the boy saw it, the fire terrified him. He had never seen anything like it before. He stood for a while, transfixed, before slowly approaching. He noticed that the flame had a piercing light and such a powerful effect that it changed anything it touched into itself. His natural daring and courage made him stretch out his hand and try to take a piece but, as soon as he touched it, the flame burned his hand and he had to let go. Then it occurred to him to pick up a firebrand. Holding it by the safe end, he carried it to the cave which he had chosen as his shelter.

He kept the fire supplied with plenty of dry grass and wood, stoking it day and night. It delighted him and increased his comfort at night by taking the place of the sun's light and warmth. He liked it enormously and thought it the best thing he had. He would watch it reaching upwards, all the time seeking height and it seemed to him like one of the jewels that sparkle in the sky.

He tested its strength against various things by putting them in the fire and watching how quickly it consumed them, depending on how strong or weak the disposition of the object was to combustion. One of the things he threw into the fire, by way of experiment, was some sort of sea-creature that had been cast up on the shore. As it cooked, the aroma spread and whetted his appetite. He ate a little, liked what he ate and as a result, got into the habit of eating meat. He took up hunting and fishing, in which he soon became expert.

The good eating he could now enjoy, which he had not experienced before, increased his liking for the fire. As his attachment to it grew stronger and he realised the extent of its potential usefulness, it occurred to him that the thing which had abandoned the heart of his mother – the gazelle who had raised him – was of the same, or a similar, substance.   His belief was confirmed by the observation, to which there are no exceptions, of the warmth of an animal's body throughout its life but its coldness after death. He noticed, too, the warmth in his own breast at the same spot he had cut open the gazelle. He thought that, if he took a live animal, cut open its heart and looked into the chamber which he had found empty when he opened his mother's heart, he would find it filled with the thing that dwells there.   Then he would be able to confirm if it was the same substance as fire and whether or not it contained heat and light.

So he captured and tied up a wild animal and cut into it as he had done with the gazelle, until he reached the heart.   He pierced the left ventricle first and discovered the chamber filled with a vapour that looked like mist.   He poked his finger inside and found it was almost hot enough to burn him. The animal expired on the spot but the boy had established to his own satisfaction that it was this warm vapour which had animated the creature and that the same thing is found in every animal. When it departs the body, the animal dies.

He then became curious to study the arrangement, location and size of the organs.   How are they connected to each other and supplied with that warm, life-giving vapour? How does the vapour remain for the length of time it does? Where does it come from? Why does its heat not dissipate?

He investigated these issues by carrying out dissections and vivi-sections, a practice he pursued so diligently and systematically that he reached a level of knowledge equivalent to that of the greatest natural scientists.

It became clear to him that every animal, even those with many organs and well-developed senses and movements, is integral and whole by virtue of that spirit whose source is one chamber, whence proceeds its distribution among the other organs. Each organ either serves the spirit or derives its function from it. The role of the spirit in activating the body is like that of his own in relation to the tools he uses to fight, hunt or dissect.

Weapons can be classified into offensive and defensive. Hunting equipment can be classified into those used to catch land animals and those used to catch fish. Dissection instruments can be classified into those for incising, those for cutting and those for fracturing.

The physical body is integral and whole and its various modes of activation are carried out in ways commensurate with the suitability of each instrument and to the extent required by the activation. Similarly, the animal spirit is integral. When it operates on the instrument of the eye, its action is sight and when it operates on the instrument of the nose, its action is smell. When it operates on the instrument of the tongue, its action is taste and on the skin, its action is touch. On the penis, its action is erection and on the liver, it is nutrition.

Every action has an organ or limb that serves it and no action can be performed unless something of the animal spirit reaches that organ along pathways, called nerves. If these pathways are cut or blocked, the organ is prevented from carrying out its function. The nerves carry the animal spirit from inside the brain, which contains a large number of spirits because of the many sections into which it is divided. The brain is itself supplied with the spirit by the heart.

If any limb or organ is deprived of the spirit, for whatever reason, it will become inactive, like a discarded tool used by no-one that has now become obsolete. Should the spirit make a complete exit from the body, become spent or somehow dissipate, the whole body will become inactive and arrive at the state of death.

By such methodical reasoning, he reached this level of insight by the end of the third septenary of his life, that is, the age of twenty-one.

At the same time, he had developed considerable ingenuity. He was making his own clothes and shoes from the hides of the animals he dissected. He made thread from their fur and strands of reed, mallow, hemp and other kinds of fibrous plants. For needles, he used thorns and splinters of cane sharpened on stones. His first steps in this direction had been with the esparto grass.

Watching swallows at work inspired him to build. He built a storehouse for his surplus food and secured it with a door of matted reeds to prevent animals intruding when he was away on other business.

He tamed birds of prey to help him hunt and fish and he domesticated hens to provide chickens and eggs. He fixed the tooth-like points from the antlers of wild antelopes to firm canes and branches and, by using fire and sharp stones, made these into spear-like weapons. He made a shield from reinforced leather. This all proceeded from the realisation that he could compensate with his hands for the natural weapons which he lacked.

None of the different species of animals now attacked him. Instead, they ran away and he found it impossible to give chase. Thinking of a way around this, it seemed to him that the best solution was to try to tame one of the wild horses or asses on the island, by feeding it food it liked. Then he could stalk the others on horseback. He selected one and, by taming it, achieved his aim. With hides fastened to the beast for a saddle and leather straps as reins, he could now hunt those animals that were difficult for him to trap.

He mastered all these skills while occupied with dissection and the study of zoology which, as I have indicated, he completed by the age of twenty-one.

*

Thereafter, another line of enquiry began to occupy him. He set out to study all the bodies in the world of formation and decay – the various species of animals and plants, varieties of minerals and stones, earth, water, steam, snow, hail, smoke, ice, flame and embers. He observed them to have many properties, different actions and analogous and contrary movements. As he deepened his inquiry, he realised that, although they shared some attributes, they differed in respect of others and that, while there was only one point of similarity, the points of dissimilarity were many and various. When he considered the properties of things and what distinguishes one from another, it seemed that there was only boundless multiplicity and that existence was far too diverse to grasp.

His own self, too, appeared to be a multiplicity. He considered each of his limbs separately and observed that, while each was characterised by a function and attribute specific to itself, it could, nevertheless, be divided into very many parts. He thus concluded that his own self was a multiplicity as, indeed, was everything else.

However, by following a second line of reasoning, he perceived all his limbs and organs, although many, to be connected and to have no clear lines of demarcation between them. They were effectively one and differed only in respect of their actions, a difference caused exclusively by the power of the animal spirit that each receives – which was the conclusion he had reached before. The spirit is integral within his own self and is the reality of the self, while all the vital organs are like tools. By this line of reasoning, he perceived of himself as whole.

He then turned his thoughts to the animals and, by the same process of reasoning, saw each individual as integral and whole. When he studied separate species, like the gazelle, horse, donkey and the varieties of birds, he realised that the individuals of each resembled one another in respect of limbs, organs, movement, behaviour and instincts. The differences between them were much less than what they had in common. This convinced him that the spirit pertaining to each species is one thing and differs only in being divided among many hearts. Were it possible to gather together in one vessel everything divided, it would be just one thing – in the same way that a single volume of water or wine, distributed among many bottles then reconstituted, is one and the same thing in either case. Its multiplicity is, in a sense, only accidental.

By this reasoning, he came to see each species as one and the multiplicity of its individuals like the multiplicity of one individual's vital parts which, in reality, are not a multiplicity at all.

He next considered all animal species together and observed them to be similar in respect of sensory perception, nutrition and the capacity for independent movement. He realised that these behaviours are unique to the working of the animal spirit and that the subsequent diversity of individual species is not markedly specific to the spirit.

Following this line of reasoning, it became apparent that the animal spirit which pertains to all species is, in reality, one, even if there are some minor differences by which any one species is distinguished. This might be likened to a volume of water distributed among many bottles; although some parts may become colder than others, they are all fundamentally the same thing. The specific association of the animal spirit to any one species is like those parts of the water which have the same degree of coldness. But otherwise, and just as the water is one, the animal spirit is one and its multiplicity is, in a sense, merely accidental. Reasoning in this way, he perceived the animal kingdom to be one.

Turning his attention next to the different species of plants, he observed that the members of any given species resemble one another in respect of branches, leaves, flowers, fruit and motion. Drawing the analogy with animals, he realised that there is one thing which all plants have in common, by virtue of which they are one, and this he likened to the former's animal spirit. The observable similarity of all plants in respect of nutrition and growth further convinced him of the unity of the plant kingdom.

He then considered the animal and plant kingdoms together and observed that they correspond in respect of nutrition and growth, although animals are superior to plants by virtue of sensory perception, intelligence and the capacity for independent movement (still, it seemed to be a possibility that plants have something approximating to this, *viz.* the turning of flowers towards the sun and the searching of roots for a source of nutrition). Reflecting in this way, animals and plants appeared to him to be one because of one thing they have in common which, in animals, is more developed and consummate and in plants has been handicapped by some impediment. This is like a single quantity of water divided into two parts, one of which freezes while the other remains liquid. Thus, in his opinion, plants and animals formed a unity.

Next, he studied objects that are not sensible, do not require nutrition and do not grow, such as stones, earth, water, air and fire, and observed them to be bodies with a measure of length, breadth and depth. Otherwise, they differ only inasmuch as some have colour that others lack, some are hot while others are cold, and differences of that sort. He observed that a hot thing could become cold and a cold thing become hot. Water becomes steam and steam becomes water. Something burning will turn into embers, ash, flame and smoke and if, as it rises, smoke makes contact with a vault of stone, it will solidify and become mineral. Reflecting on this, it seemed that they are all one thing in reality, even if multiplicity attaches to them accidentally, as it does to animals and plants.

Thinking about what might constitute the unity of animals and plants, he understood that it was a body with length, breadth and depth, that can be either hot or cold, just like an inanimate body that has no sensory perception and no nutritional requirements. It differs only by virtue of actions, as displayed through animal and plant limbs. However, if these actions are not essential but are endowed by something else and if inanimate bodies were similarly endowed, would they be the same? He considered the animate body essentially, abstracted from the actions which he had first thought emanated from it, and perceived it to be just another body. He realised that all bodies, animate or inanimate, motile or inert, are one thing, although it is obvious that some display instrumental actions. He remained unclear whether these actions are essential or contingent.

He had thus reached a point where he thought that there was nothing other than bodies and that while existence, by one line of reasoning, was a limitless and infinite multiplicity by another, it was only one thing. He would remain in this position for some time.

He then considered all animate and inanimate bodies (which, at times, seemed to be one thing and at other times, infinitely many) and decided that one of two conditions must apply to each: either it moves in an upwards direction, like smoke and flame or air when released under water, or it moves in the opposite, downwards, direction, like water and animal, mineral and vegetable parts. No body is free from one of these two movements and, consequently, each body remains at rest only if something obstructs its path. For example, a falling stone that strikes the ground cannot pass on through but if it could, it appears that it would never stop moving. If you pick up the stone, you find it offering resistance because of its downwards-seeking tendency. Similarly, smoke continues to rise until it comes into contact with the roof, whereupon it twists and turns around. If it escapes, it rises up through the air since air cannot confine it. He observed that if a water-skin is filled with air, tied and then submerged under water, it will continue to offer resistance and seek to rise until it emerges from the water and reaches the level of the air, whereupon it comes to rest and the upwards tendency and resistance it previously displayed disappear.

He set out to discover whether there was a body that, at any given time, was free from both of these movements and the tendency, while stationary, towards one or other direction. His aim was to find such a body and examine its nature, as a body, without the attachment of any attribute, since attributes are the source of multiplicity. He found nothing like that among the bodies around him but, contemplating those with the smallest number of attributes, he observed that nothing was without one of two attributes, expressible as gravity and levity. Do these, he wondered, pertain to the body itself or to a concept additional to that of corporeity?

It appeared that they must pertain to a concept additional to corporeity because, if they pertained to the body by the mere fact of its being a body, they would both pertain to all bodies. However, we find a heavy object without levity and a light one without gravity although both are, undeniably, bodies. Each possesses a concept additional to its corporeity that uniquely distinguishes it from the other and without which, the two would be the same in all respects.

It thus became clear that the reality of heavy and light objects is composed of two concepts. The first is what each has in common, namely the attribute of corporeity, and the second is what distinguishes the reality of one from the other, *i.e.* gravity in one case and levity in the other. These adhere to the concept of corporeity and are the attributes which cause one to move downwards and the other to move upwards. Having studied all animate and inanimate bodies, he concluded that the existential reality of each was, similarly, a composite of the concept of corporeity and one or more things additional to its corporeity.

He thus became aware of the different forms[30] of bodies. This was his first intimation of the world of the spirit, since forms are not perceived by the senses but by a kind of intellectualisation.

His researches showed that the animal spirit – whose location is the heart he had dissected initially – must also possess some concept over and above its corporeity, adapting it to perform the unique range of actions (*i.e.* sensations, feelings and movements) which characterise it. That concept is its form and the criterion by which it is distinguished from other bodies. It is what philosophers call "the animal soul". Similarly, the thing which, in plants, takes the place of natural animal warmth has its own, unique quality and is called by philosophers "the vegetative soul". All inanimate bodies – *i.e.* everything other than animals and plants in the world of formation and decay – have something specific to them that produces the characteristic action of each, such as its direction of motion and what can be perceived by the senses about it. That thing is the criterion of each and is what philosophers refer to as "nature".

When he had thus reasoned that the reality of the animal spirit, which had fascinated him for so long, consists of the concept of corporeity and a concept additional to corporeity and that, while corporeity is common to all bodies, it is this other concept adhering to it which distinguishes them, he dismissed corporeity as unimportant. What now interested him was this other concept (called "the soul") and he became eager for accurate knowledge of it.

He began an examination of all bodies, not from the aspect of corporeity, but from the aspect of the essential forms which entail the specific characteristics that distinguish one body from another. Focusing on this line of enquiry, he perceived there to be one set of bodies with a common form, from which one or more actions derives. Within that set, he identified a category sharing the form of the set but possessing an additional form from which other actions derive. Within that category, he identified a class sharing the first and second form with the category but having a third form from which certain specific actions also derive.

For example, all terrestrial bodies – soil, stones, minerals, plants, animals and other bodies with gravity – constitute one set, sharing one form from which movement in a downwards direction, unless otherwise impeded, derives. When forcibly raised upwards and let go of, they move downwards by virtue of their form.

Within that set, there is a category – plants and animals – that possesses the first form in common with the set but has an additional form from which nutrition and growth derive. Nutrition consists in the subject replacing bodily depletion by taking to itself material similar to its own substance and transforming it into that substance. Growth is a consistent and proportional increase in the body's dimensions (its height, width and depth) as a consequence of the nutrition it receives. These two actions apply generally to plants and animals and clearly derive from a common form, *i.e.* the vegetative soul.

A class within this category – animals – shares the first two forms with the category but has an additional, third form from which derive sensory perceptions and the capacity for independent movement from place to place.

The characteristic feature of each animal species, which uniquely distinguishes it from other species derives, he realised, from a form specific to it alone and additional to the concept of the form it shares with other species. Each species of plant is distinguished in a similar way.

It thus appeared that the reality of perceptible bodies in the world of formation and decay is a composite, in some cases of many concepts additional to corporeity, in other cases of few.

Appreciating that to understand what is few is easier than to understand what is many, he put aside consideration of the forms of animals and plants for the moment, since they are complex compounds of many concepts because of their many and varied actions, and sought to examine the reality of the simplest compounds. Aware that some minerals are simpler than others, he looked for the simplest. He thought, too, that water, fire and air had simple compositions, because of the small number of actions to which their forms give rise.

He had previously concluded that these four elements are capable of being transformed into one another and that they have one thing in common – the concept of corporeity – which is necessarily free from the concepts by which each of the four is individually characterised. This thing cannot move upwards or downwards, be hot or cold, wet or dry, since none of these attributes is generally applicable to all bodies. These attributes cannot, therefore, pertain to the body *qua* body since, were it possible for a body to exist without a form additional to that of its corporeity, it would possess none of these attributes. It is impossible for a body to possess an attribute that cannot be generalised to each and every formal body.

He tried to discover one attribute that is generally applicable to all bodies, animate or inanimate, and concluded that only the concept of mass,[31] expressible as length, breadth and depth, applies to each. He understood that this concept pertains to the body by the very fact of its being a body but could not perceive by sense the existence of any body with this attribute alone in such a way that it possessed nothing additional to the said mass and was thus wholly devoid of other forms.

He considered mass. Is it the very concept of corporeity itself or is it a superimposed concept? He then realised that, beyond mass, there is another concept which, as it cannot exist by itself, mass alone exists in –

i.e. something with mass cannot exist without also having three dimensions.

He took the example of clay as a perceptible and formal body and observed that, if shaped into a ball, it has a degree of length, breadth and depth. If the ball is then reshaped into a cube or an oval, its length, breadth and depth are altered accordingly. The clay itself remains unchanged but can never be devoid of some degree of length, breadth and depth. However, the fact that the clay's dimensions can be successively altered make it clear that mass is a concept distinct from the clay itself, although one which, because the clay cannot be free from it, is a part of its reality.

Reasoning in this way, he concluded that each and every body, as a body, is composed in reality of two concepts, one as the clay in relation to the ball in the above example and the other, as the length, breadth and depth of the ball or cube or whatever shape the clay may be. Each and every body can only be understood as a compound of these two, mutually dependent, concepts. The one that can be changed and successively altered in various ways is the concept of mass and pertains to all formal bodies, while the one which remains in a fixed state – as the clay in the above example – is the concept of corporeity which, likewise, pertains to all formal bodies. The thing represented in the above example by the clay is what metaphysicians call *matter,* or *hyle,* and it is completely devoid of form.

When his reasoning had led him to the point where he had, to some extent, transcended sensory perception and now surveyed the foothills of the intellectual world, he felt quite lost and longed for the familiarity of the world of the senses. However, he took stock for a while then put that world firmly behind him. What he was now engaged upon could not be grasped by sensory perception.

Taking the four simplest, perceptible bodies he knew of, he first considered water, observing that, if allowed to remain as its form demands, it is perceptibly cool and tends to descent. If heated by fire or the sun, the coolness vanishes but the downwards tendency remains until, after further application of heat, it begins to tend upwards. The two constant and characteristic emanations of its form thus disappear entirely. His understanding of its form consisted exclusively of the emanation of these two actions and when these vanish, the form disintegrates. The aqueous form of water thus disappears from the body when actions which derive essentially from another form are displayed.   Another, previously non-existent, form is brought about and actions are then displayed that, by their nature, could not be displayed by the body while remaining in its initial form.

Understanding that, for everything that is brought about, there must necessarily be something which brings it about, he formed a general, as yet vague, impression of there being an efficient cause of the form.

One by one, he re-examined all the forms of which he was aware and concluded that each was brought into being and must therefore have an efficient cause.   He perceived the essence of any given form to be no more than the disposition of the respective body to display a particular action.   Water, for example, has a disposition and an aptitude to motion in an upwards   direction if sufficient heat is applied. That very disposition is its form, since there is otherwise only a body, previously non-existent things such as texture and motion that the senses can perceive about the body and an efficient cause that brings these about. The aptitude of the body for certain movements rather than others is its disposition and form, and this clearly holds true for all forms. He therefore concluded that the actions which emanate from forms do not, in fact, pertain to them but to an efficient cause that animates, through them, the actions attributed to them.

This is the idea expressed by the Prophet when he said, "I am His hearing by which He hears and His sight by which He sees" and by the Decisive Revelation, *It was not you who destroyed them but the Lord, nor you who struck them down but Him.*[32]

Having thus grasped the general idea of an efficient cause, his desire for more precise knowledge quickened. He had still not transcended the physical world and it was at the level of sensory perception that he began searching for this efficient cause, as yet unaware whether it was one or many.

He considered all the bodies around him (the same ones he always considered) and perceived them to be at all times in a state of either formation or decay. Whatever did not suffer total decay suffered decay of its parts. Water and earth, for example, could be partially degraded by fire. Likewise, air could be degraded by extreme cold and form water and ice. No bodies within his experience were either not originated or did not suppose an efficient cause.

Now leaving this aside, he turned his attention to the celestial bodies, being then at the end of the fourth septenary of his life, that is, at the age of twenty-eight.

*

He knew that the sky and all the stars it contains are bodies because they possess the three dimensions of length, breadth and depth and these are inseparable from them. Anything from which the attribute of mass cannot be separated is a body and, therefore, they, too, must be bodies.

He then wondered whether the mass of the cosmos extends to infinity in all directions, or whether it is finite and limited by defined boundaries beyond which mass is impossible. This point confused him initially but, by the power of his reasoning and innate intelligence, he came to the conclusion that a body of infinite size is a practical and theoretical impossibility, *i.e.* an absurdity. He established this to his own satisfaction with numerous arguments and proofs, of which the following is an example:

"I have no doubt that, in the region closest to me and of which I am aware, the cosmos is finite because I can see it with my own eyes. In the other direction – and this is what has caused some doubt – I also know that it is impossible for it to extend to infinity.

Imagine two lines beginning from where it is known to be finite and extending infinitely with and through the mass of the cosmos. Then imagine a long section cut from one of these lines at its finite end. Take the remainder and place the end which was cut beside the beginning of the intact line so that the two lines lie in parallel. Now consider these two lines as they extend into supposed infinity.

Either we find that both lines extend forever into infinity with neither being shorter than the other, in which case the line from which the section was removed is equal to the line which remained intact – and that is impossible – or we find that the line from which the section was removed does not extend indefinitely with the intact line but stops short, in which case it is finite. If the finite section that was initially removed is then replaced, the whole, likewise, becomes finite although it is neither shorter nor longer than the other, intact, line but is, in fact, the same. It therefore follows that both lines are finite.

The body on which these lines were supposed is also finite and, because we can suppose lines like these on any body, all bodies are finite. The supposition that a body can be infinite is, therefore, absurd."[33]

When the subtlety of his thinking had demonstrated, by arguments such as this, that the cosmos is finite, he was anxious to know what shape it was and what its boundary conditions might be.

He first considered the sun, moon and stars and observed how they all rise in the east and set in the west. Those passing overhead, he observed, describe a wider arc than those inclining to the north or south. The further from the zenith, in either direction, the shorter the trajectory, so that the shortest stellar arcs are two – the orbit of Canopus around the south pole and that of the Guardians of the Pole[34] around the north pole. He lived, as we have said, on the equator and all these orbits thus appeared above his horizon. Analogous conditions pertained to the north and south and both polar orbits were visible simultaneously. While one star might rise on a wide arc and another on a small arc, he nevertheless observed that, if both rose together, they set together. This appeared to be the case with all stars, at all times.

Consequently, the firmament appeared to be spherical in shape and he confirmed this theory by observing that the sun, moon and stars return to the east after setting in the west and by observing that they seem to be the same size when they rise, reach their median and set.[35] If their motion was not orbital, they would be visibly closer at certain times and appear to vary in size. As this was not so, he concluded positively that the firmament is spherical in shape.

He studied carefully the motion of the moon and observed that it regresses towards the east, as do the planets.[36]

With the wide knowledge of astronomy he had acquired, it seemed to him that the planetary and stellar movements consisted of a number of spheres, all governed by one supreme sphere which moves the entire firmament from east to west [to east] in the course of a day and a night. The explanation of how this shift takes place is a lengthy subject and, as it has been fully dealt with in the literature, there is no need for us to say more here.

When he came to understand this, he realised that the universe and everything it contains is as one thing in which everything is connected. All the bodies he had studied – earth, water, air, plants, animals etc. – are integral to it and resemble, to some extent, an individual animal. The shining stars are like the senses of the animal and the synchronised planetary orbits are like its limbs and organs. The contents of the world of formation and decay can be likened to the vapours and waste inside the an animal's belly, in which living creatures are often formed, as they are in the macrocosm. The universe was, in reality, like one individual whose many parts formed a unity, he believed, by analogy with the unity of bodies in the world of formation and decay.

*

He then concentrated his thoughts on the universe as a whole. Is it something originated in time that emerged into being from non-being, or something that was never preceded by non-being but has always existed?

He was uncertain of the answer to this and unable to reach a definite conclusion one way or the other. If he assumed belief in pre-eternality, many objections emerged concerning the impossibility of infinite existence, by analogy with the impossibility of the existence of a body of infinite size. He also observed that the universe is not devoid of originated phenomena that it could not have preceded. Whatever cannot have preceded such phenomena must itself be originated.

However, other contradictions arose if he assumed belief in the origination of the universe. The concept of origination in time subsequent to non-being is incomprehensible unless the universe was preceded by time. Time, however, pertains inseparably to the universe, therefore it is incomprehensible that the universe be subsequent to time. His thinking continued,

"If the universe was originated, it must have an originator. Why has this originator brought the universe into being now and not at some time in the past? How could it have been brought into being as a result of some external force acting upon the originator, if there was nothing else in existence? And if it was brought into being by some spontaneous change occurring in the originator, what could have caused the change?"

He speculated on these issues for several years, his mind filled with contradictory and opposing arguments and unable to decide conclusively one way or the other. Frustrated, he then began to think about what the implications of each of these beliefs were and whether, perhaps, they might be the same.

If he supposed the origination of the universe and its coming into being after non-being, it necessarily followed that it could not have come into being by itself but must have been brought into being by an agent. It is impossible to perceive this agent with any of the senses because it would then be just another body, in which case it would be part of the universe, originated and itself requiring an originator. If this second originator was also a body, there would have to be a third originator then a fourth and so on, *ad infinitum*, which is absurd.

The universe must, therefore, have a non-corporeal agent that cannot be perceived by the senses, since the five senses perceive only bodies or what attaches to bodies. If it is impossible to perceive with the senses, it will also be impossible to perceive with the imagination, because imagination is simply a representation of the forms of things perceived by the senses when the things themselves are no longer present. If the agent is non-corporeal, it will be impossible to apply the attributes of corporeity to it and, therefore, it must be free from the principal attribute of corporeity – mass – and all subsequent corporeal attributes. And if the universe has an agent, it must have perfect knowledge and mastery of the universe. *Does He, the Subtle and Omniscient, not know His own creation?*[37]

If he then supposed the universe to be pre-eternal, never preceded by non-being and having always been, it followed that its motion must be pre-eternal and infinite in respect of beginning, since no preceding state of stasis existed from which it might have begun.

Now, for every motion there must necessarily be a propelling force. This propelling force may either be distributed throughout the body – whether the moving body itself or one external to it – or be undistrib-uted.   Any force distributed within a body can be divided in proportion as the body is divided and multiplied as it is multiplied. For example, gravity in a stone causes it to move downwards. If the stone is divided in two, its weight is divided in two. If a similar stone is placed on top, the weight is increased proportionately.   Were it possible to keep adding stones indefinitely, the weight would increase indefinitely and, if the number of stones reached a limit beyond which no more could be added, the weight would, likewise, reach its limit.

Given that each and every body is finite, so each and every force within a body must also be finite. Therefore, if we discover a force that causes an event of infinite duration, it must be a non-corporeal force. We have found the universe to be in constant and infinite motion, since we have supposed it to be pre-eternal and without beginning. It therefore follows that the force which moves it is neither within its body nor one external to it but must pertain to something independent of corporeality, to which corporeal attributes may not be applied.

His initial reasoning about the world of formation and decay had demonstrated that the existential reality of each body lies in its disposition, by virtue of its form, to certain movements and that its existence in respect of substance is weak and barely perceptible. In that case, the existence of the entire universe must consist in its disposition to the momentum of this propelling force, itself transcendent of matter and devoid of corporeal attributes, beyond the perception of the senses or grasp of the imagination. Such a constant, tireless and inexhaustible agent of the many and varied motions of the spheres must necessarily have total mastery and be all-knowing.   May He be praised!   Thus he arrived at the same conclusion that he had by his first line of reasoning.

Uncertainty over the sempiternity or origination of the universe now no longer troubled him, since both propositions demonstrate the existence of a non-corporeal agent that is neither attached to a body nor separate, neither within a body nor without. Attachment and separation, within and without are all predicates of bodies and of these He is devoid.

Since the matter of each body requires form, without which it cannot exist or establish a reality, and the existence of the form is inadmissible without the action of this agent, it is clear that all existing things require this agent for their existence. Nothing could exist without Him.   He is their cause and they, His effect, irrespective of whether they were brought into being from non-being or were never preceded by non-being and are without beginning in respect of time. In either case, they are caused by and assume an agent on whom they depend for their existence. Without His permanence they would not remain, without His existence they would not exist and without His pre-eternality they would not be pre-eternal.   Yet He is essentially free from and independent of them. How could it be otherwise when it has been established that His power and command are infinite but that all existing things and everything joined or attached to them, however loosely, are clearly finite?

The whole universe, then, and everything within – the earth, sky, planets and stars and everything between and above and beneath them – is His work and His creation and consequent to Him in essence, although not subsequent in respect of time. Imagine yourself holding some object in your hand then moving your hand, the object will move in keeping with the movement of your hand. Its motion will be consequent, in essence, upon the motion of your hand but not subsequent to it in time, since the two motions began together. Similarly, the entire universe is the Creator's effect and creation, out of time. *His command is such that if He wants a thing to be, all that He need say is "Be!" and it will be.*[38]

When he realised that all existence is His work, he looked at all things differently thereafter, in recognition of the power of the Creator and with wonder at the mystery of His work, the subtlety of His wisdom and the precision of His knowledge. He saw in the smallest things, quite apart from the largest, traces of wisdom and subtlety that caused him wonder and which, he understood, could issue only from a Creator of ultimate perfection, indeed beyond perfection. *Neither in the heavens nor on earth does the weight of a speck of dust, or anything greater or less, escape His notice.*[39]

He meditated on how He gave each animal species its creation and its guidance. Without His guidance, no animal could use as He intended the limbs He gave it, which would instead be burdensome. He realised then that He is the Most Generous and Compassionate.

Whenever he now saw anything beautiful or good, consummate or strong – or any fine thing he stopped to reflect and realised that it emanated from the existence and the work of the Creator, may He be praised! He understood that what is within His essence is much greater and more perfect, more complete and more beautiful, more splendid, more lovely and more lasting, far beyond compare. Meditating on the attributes of perfection, he found them all to be His and to issue from Him. It is He who is more deserving to be so described.

Considering the attributes of imperfection, he knew that He is free from and devoid of them. How could it be otherwise when the very concept of imperfection is absolute non-being or something that attaches to non-being? How can non-being attach to or enshroud He who is Absolute Being, whose existence is essentially necessary, the One who gives all existing things their being and without whom there is no existence. He is

Being, He is Perfection, He is the Absolute, He is the Good, He is the Power, He is the Glory, He is the Knowledge. He is. *And all things shall perish except His countenance.*

He reached this level of understanding by the end of the fifth septenary of his life, that is, at the age of thirty-five. His heart become so in thrall to the Agent that he thought of nothing but Him. He lost interest in the study of things. He reached the stage where he had only to look at something to see at once the trace of His work, whereupon his thoughts transferred to the Maker and abandoned the artefact. His longing for Him became so intense that his heart, in its attachment to the world of the intellect, found the entire physical world nothing but vexation.

*

When he became aware of this Sublime Being, whose existence is constant and without cause and is the cause of the being of all things, he wished to understand how he had acquired such a knowledge and with what faculty he had perceived of Him.

He first considered each of his senses -- hearing, sight, smell, taste and touch -- which, he knew, could only perceive a body or something within a body. The sense of hearing, for example, only perceives what is audible, *i.e.* the vibration of air that results from bodies coming into contact. The sense of sight perceives colours, smell perceives odours, taste perceives flavours and touch perceives temperature and texture. Similarly, the faculty of imagination perceives nothing without length, breadth and depth. The senses can perceive nothing other than these attributes of bodies because, as faculties distributed within bodies, they are divisible only as bodies are divisible. If a faculty that is distributed within something divisible perceives an object, the object itself must be divisible as the faculty is divisible. Every bodily faculty can, therefore, perceive only something divisible, *i.e.* a body or something within a body.

Now, it is clear that the Necessarily Existent Being is entirely devoid of corporeal attributes. There is, therefore, no way to perceive Him with something that is itself a body, a bodily faculty, connected in some way to a body, intrinsic or extrinsic to a body, attached to or detached from a body.

It was clear to him that he had become aware of this Being with his self and that the knowledge he had of Him was firm and fast. It therefore appeared that the self, with which he had perceived, was something non-corporeal, admitting none of the attributes of corporeity. The external, corporeal aspect he perceived of himself was not his true self. His true self was the thing with which he had perceived the Necessarily Existent Being.

Realising that his self was not the tangible body he perceived with the senses and which was enclosed in skin, he viewed his whole body with indifference. He set about the contemplation of that sublime self by which he had become aware of the Sublime & Necessarily Existent Being.

Considering his self, he wondered whether it is possible for it to decay, perish and disappear or whether it is eternal. He knew that transience and decay are attributes of bodies, whereby one form is cast of and another put on, like water becoming air and air becoming water, or plants turning to earth and dust which, in turn, become plants. Such is the meaning of decay. But something non-corporeal, having no need of the body for its existence and completely devoid of any aspect of corporeity, cannot possibly be imagined to decay.

Thus establishing the impossibility that his true self decay, he wished to know what its condition would be when it shrugged off the body and departed. He had already realised that it would do so only when the body was no longer a suitable instrument for it.

Considering the faculties of sensory perception again, he realised that each, at different times, could be in a state of actual and potential perception. For example, when the eye is closed or otherwise prevented from seeing, it is in a state of potential perception — *i.e.*, it is not perceiving now but may perceive at some time in the future. If the eye is opened and becomes receptive to what can be seen, it is in a state of actual perception — *i.e.*, it is now perceiving. Each faculty can similarly be in a state of actual and potential perception. Had any faculty never actually perceived then, while it remained potentially perceptive, no desire would be felt for the objects of its specific perception since these would, as yet, be unfamiliar — take the case of a man blind from birth. However, if what had once been actual perception became potential then, for as long as it remained so, a strong desire for actual perception would be felt, since it was an experience to which one had once been accustomed. The sighted man who becomes blind, for example, never stops longing to see again.

The more consummate, beautiful and good the perceived thing may be, the greater the desire for it and the distress at its loss. Accordingly, the distress of someone who has lost his sight is sharper than that of someone who has lost his sense of smell, since the things perceived by sight are more consummate and beautiful than those perceived by smell.

If it were possible for there to be something infinitely perfect and beautiful and good, something beyond perfection, beauty and goodness (and there is no perfection or beauty or goodness in existence except as emanates radiantly from Him) then whoever lost the perception of that thing, having once known it, would surely remain in infinite suffering for as long as he was deprived of it. However, someone perceiving such a thing constantly would remain in endless rapture, perfect delight and infinite comfort and bliss.

It was already clear to him that the Necessarily Existent Being, attributed with all the qualities of perfection, is devoid of and free from the attributes of imperfection. He was certain, too, that the thing with which he had come to perceive Him neither resembles bodies nor decays as bodies do. It therefore seemed that, upon departing the body at death, one of three conditions could apply to the being with the kind of self disposed to such perception.

Firstly, if, during the time in which he had quickened the body prior to death, a man had experienced no awareness of the Necessarily Existent Being, had never aspired to Him and had never even heard of Him then, upon departing the body, that man will neither long for the Being nor suffer at the loss of Him. All bodily faculties cease to function when the body stops working, so neither will he long for the demands of those faculties nor suffer their deprivation. Such is the condition of all dumb animals, in human form or otherwise.

Secondly, if a man had known of the Necessarily Existent Being prior to death and recognised His perfection, power, majesty, glory and goodness but had turned away from Him and followed his passions until, in that state death surprised him, he would be denied witness yet long for it and remain in endless torment and infinite suffering. He might, after much effort, release himself from suffering and bear witness to the object of his longing or he may continue suffering for all eternity, according to the disposition of character he had possessed during his bodily existence.

Thirdly, if a man knew of the Necessarily Existent Being prior to slipping off the mortal coil and had devoted himself wholly unto Him and to the contemplation of His majesty, goodness and splendour, from which he did not turn aside before death, he would be in a state of actual devotion and witness. On departing the body, he will remain in infinite joy and constant rapture, delight and bliss at the continuity of his witness to the Necessarily Existent Being and the clear, unspoilt integrity of that witness. The sensory demands of the body which, to that state, bring only distraction, drudgery and pain, will disappear.

It was, therefore clear that the perfection of his self and its happiness lay exclusively in bearing actual and constant witness to the Necessarily Existent Being undistracted, even momentarily, unto death. And, dying in the condition of actual witness, his rapture might continue forever, unimpaired by suffering.

He then began to consider how he might make this actual and constant witness in such a way that he would not turn aside or be distracted. He thought of the Being at all times but when anything cut across his field of vision or the sound of an animal pierced his ears, some fantasy or physical pain distracted him, if he became hungry or thirsty, hot or cold, or needed to pay a call of nature, his concentration was disturbed and, afterwards, he found it hard to recollect his thoughts and recommence his meditation upon the state of witness. He was afraid of dying suddenly while in a state of distraction and so fall into eternal unhappiness and suffer the pain of exclusion. This disturbed and vexed him but the remedy was elusive.

Thinking he might learn from them the means of his own salvation, he studied the actions and behaviour of animals, to see whether some, perhaps, displayed any awareness of the Being and any aspiration towards Him. However, he observed them all to be occupied with nothing more than finding food and drink, satisfying sexual appetite and seeking warmth or shade. Thus do they carry on day and night until their time is up and they pass away. He saw none that followed a different path or that ever looked for anything else. Clearly, they have no awareness and no longing for the Being whatsoever; they are all destined for non-being or some similar state.

Judging that to be the case with animals, he realised that it would be even more so with plants, since they possess not even a fraction of animals' perception. If the more perceptive has not achieved any sort of awareness, it is unlikely that the less perceptive will have. Besides, he noticed that the actions of plants amount to no more than ingestion and generation.

He looked at the planets and stars and observed their ordered and harmonious movements. He watched them as they sparkled and shone, strangers to change and decay and felt intuitively that they possess essences, other than their bodies, that are aware of the Necessarily Existent Being. These cognisant essences are not corporeal or impressed on a body, like his cognisant essence. How could they be like him, just another decaying body, with his weakness and powerful need for sensation? Nevertheless, and despite his imperfection, his own self was still something devoid of corporeity and not subject to decay. It was just that the celestial bodies seemed somehow more worthy. He believed them to have knowledge of the Necessarily Existent Being and to bear actual and constant witness to Him because the obstacles to his constant witness were of the senses, which the celestial bodies do not possess. Why, he wondered, should he, alone among the animals, possess a self that is bestowed with some resemblance to the celestial bodies?

He had observed from the transformation of the elements into one another that nothing on the face of the earth remains in one form but is, instead, subject to a constant succession of formation and decay. Most bodies are compounds of opposing things and, for that reason, tend to decay. There is nothing pure, unalloyed and flawless, and anything that comes close is remote from decay – gold and sapphire, for example. The celestial bodies are simple and pure and that is what makes them remote from decay and successive changes of form.

He had observed that, among the totality of bodies in the world of formation and decay, there are those whose reality exists in only one form additional to the concept of corporeity. These are the four primary elements of earth, water, fire and air. Then there are bodies whose reality exists in a greater number of forms, such as animals and plants. The fewer forms of which the reality of a body consists, the fewer are its actions and the further the body is from life. In the complete absence of form, the body has no way towards life and tends to a state of semi-non-being. The more forms of which a body's reality consists, the more will be its actions and more consummate its entry into the state of life. If those forms are such that there is no way for them to leave the matter to which they pertain, life will then be at its fullest, most evident and vigorous.

Matter, or hyle, is absolutely formless, with no trace of life and is quasi-non-existent. The four primary elements exist in one form only, on the lowest level of existence in the world of formation and decay. From them, things with multiple forms are composed. Life is very weak in the four primary elements because they possess only one movement and each has an opposite that constantly resists what its nature demands and seeks to replace its form. Its existence is thus insecure and its life is weak. Life is stronger in plants and yet more evident in animals.

In compounds where the nature of one primary element dominates the others and renders them inactive, that element becomes the controlling force and the compound has only a small claim on life, since the element itself has only a small and weak claim on life. However, in compounds where the nature of no one primary element dominates but all the constituent elements are adequately balanced, with forces equal and offset in such a way that the compound bears only a remote resemblance to any one element, it is as if the form has no opposition and the compound will, accordingly, make its claim on life. The more perfect the balance becomes and the more distant from bias, the less likely the compound is to have opposition and so will its life be fuller. The animal spirit, located in the heart, is extremely well-balanced by virtue of being more subtle than earth and water but coarser than fire and air. Maintaining a state of equilibrium where it is not obviously opposed by any one of the primary elements, it thus disposes to the animal form. It follows that the most balanced animal spirit will be disposed to the most consummate life in the world of formation and decay. It might almost be said that such a spirit will have no opposition to its form and, consequently, resemble the celestial bodies which themselves have no opposition to their forms.

Because the spirit of such an animal occupies a central position between the primary elements, it will lack the absolute tendency to either upwards or downwards motion. In fact, were it possible to place it equidistantly between the base of a fire and the highest point a rising flame reaches before degrading, it would remain there and tend neither up nor down. Were it to move in space, it would orbit around a central point, as the celestial bodies do, and were it to move *in situ*, it would rotate on its own axis. It could not be other than spherical in shape. It must, therefore, closely resemble the celestial bodies.

He had already considered the condition of animals and seen nothing to suggest that they were aware of the Necessarily Existent Being, but he knew that his own self was aware. He thus became convinced that he was the animal with that balanced spirit which most resembles the celestial bodies.   It seemed to him he was distinct from other animals, created for a different purpose and prepared for some great undertaking that was not for them.

He felt honoured that even the baser of his two parts, the corporeal, resembles more than any other thing the celestial jewels which are external to the world of formation and decay and free from the phenomena of transformation, imperfection and change – while his higher part was the cognisant thing by which he had become aware of the Necessarily Existent Being and was something sovereign, immutable and holy to which decay does not attach.   It cannot be qualified by any of the attributes of bodies and does not perceive with the senses or the power of imagination. It reaches knowledge with no instrument other than itself, by which it also knows itself. It is at once the knower, the knowing and the knowledge, the intellect, the intellectualising and the intelligible. There is no distinction between any of these, since difference and distinction are attributes of bodies and bodily attachments and here there is no body, no bodily attribute and no bodily attachment.

When he had understood how his resemblance to the celestial bodies distinguished him from the other animals, he realised that he should model himself upon those bodies, imitate their movements and do his utmost to identify with them.   Believing that his higher part, the part by which he knew of the Necessarily Existent Being, possessed some resemblance to Him inasmuch as, like Him,   it is devoid of corporeal attributes, he also realised that he should strive as he could to acquire His qualities for himself.   He should create His nature in himself and model His actions.   He should devote himself to the execution of His will and surrender himself wholly to Him.   His heart should outwardly and inwardly accept all His wisdom and take its pleasure therein. And this, even if it hurt or damaged him or brought about the ruin of his body.

Nevertheless, he   acknowledged his resemblance to the other animals by virtue of that base part of him which is of the world of formation and decay – his body, oppressive and heavy, on which the senses made demands for food, drink and sex. At the same time, he did not believe that his body was created in vain or attached to him without purpose. He was obliged to look after and take care of it and this he could only do in ways that resembled animal behaviour.

The kinds of activities he had to perform were, therefore, directed towards three objectives: identification with the dumb animals, identification with the celestial bodies and identification with the Necessarily Existent Being.

The first was necessary inasmuch as he had an oppressive body, with individual limbs and organs, distinct functions and various instincts. The second was necessary because he possessed the animal spirit, located in the heart as the principal part of the body and source of its faculties. The third was necessary by virtue of his being who he is, *i.e.* the self which knows of the Necessarily Existent Being.

At first, he had thought that his happiness and triumph over suffering lay solely in bearing constant, undiminished witness to the Necessarily Existent Being but, reflecting on how he might achieve this constancy, he concluded that he had to apply himself to each of these three categories of imitative actions.

The first would bring him no closer to witness and would even distract and inhibit him since it is a digression into sensory matters and all sensory matters veil and obscure direct witness. Although there was an element of risk, necessity demanded he take this course as a means of maintaining the animal spirit in order to achieve the second kind of self-identification, with the celestial bodies.

The second would bring him a great share of constant witness but a witness nevertheless flawed. Whoever bears witness in this way alone will remain conscious of, and be distracted by, his own self, as we shall see later.

Immaculate witness and complete, undistracted absorption in the Necessarily Existent Being, is achieved by the third kind of self-identification. The self of one who bears this witness passes away and vanishes, as do all essences, be they many or few, except the Divine Essence[40] of the One, the True, the Necessarily Existent. His alone is the power and the glory.

He understood that his ultimate aim was this third kind of assimilation but that he would be unable to achieve it without a long period of discipline spent practising the second, which itself could only be sustained by means of the first. The first kind of activity would inhibit his self and help him to achieve his aim only contingently, not essentially. He therefore committed himself to it only to the extent that was necessary and sufficient to sustain the animal spirit and no more.

There were two aspects to this. The first was internal sustenance – nutrition – to compensate for bodily depletion and the second was external protection and defence against the ravages of heat, cold and rain, dangerous animals and the like.

He recognised that, were he to satisfy his needs at random, as things happened to present themselves, it would be possible to slip into excess and, by taking more than what was necessary, inadvertently frustrate his intent. He therefore decided to set limits and quantities he would not exceed. Specifically, he had to decide what sorts of food to eat, in what quantities and at what intervals.

He first considered the sorts of food and reckoned them to be three: plants that had not fully developed and matured, *i.e.* varieties of young vegetables and herbs, nuts, the soft fruits of plants whose growth was complete and which had produced seeds to propagate their kind, and edible creatures of the land and sea.

It was true that each of these was the work of the Necessarily Existent Being, in closeness and identification with whom, it was evident, lay his happiness. It was inevitable that taking them for food would deny their full development and come between them and their ultimate purpose. That in itself would be an obstruction of the Creator's work and contrary to the closeness and identification that he sought. He believed that, were it possible, the proper course would be to refrain from eating altogether. That, however, could not be, since it would lead to the decay of his own body which would be an even greater act of transgression against his Creator since he was superior to those things whose decay was the cause of his survival. So he chose the lesser of two evils and more tolerable of two transgressions.

In times of shortage, he reckoned, he should take the most readily available of these three sorts, in quantities that will be indicated below. In times of plenty, he had to decide what was a lesser transgression against the Creator's work to consume, and choose accordingly – for example, ripe, seed-bearing fruits but on condition that he take care of the seeds and neither eat them nor waste them by throwing them onto salty, stony or otherwise infertile soil. If unable to find edible, soft fruits such as apples, pears and plums, he would allow himself to take edible nuts, like walnuts and chestnuts, or young vegetables and herbs that were not fully grown. In both cases, he made it a condition to take only the most plentiful and those which reproduced the fastest and neither to tear them up by the roots nor to waste any seeds. If these were unavailable, it would be permissible to eat animals or eggs but on condition that he take only the most numerous and not eradicate any species.

This, then, was his thinking on the kinds of food he might eat. As regards quantity, he believed he should eat only enough to stave off the pangs of hunger and no more. As to intervals between meals, he thought that, once he had eaten, he should eat no more until he felt too weak to perform the duties required by the second kind of self-identification, which will be described below.

The need for external protection to sustain the animal spirit was a simple matter, since he dressed in animal hides and already had a shelter to protect against the elements. He believed that was sufficient and saw no reason to bother himself further. He then committed himself to the dietary rules he had drawn up, as detailed above.

He next considered the second kind of activity, namely identification with, and imitation of, the celestial bodies, the adoption of their qualities and acquisition of their attributes. He categorised these attributes into three types.

The first consists of those they possess that affect the world below of formation and decay, such as the provision of heat by essence and cold by contingency, of light, rarefaction and condensation, and other conditions which they produce whereby the world is made receptive to the radiant emanation of spiritual forms from the Necessarily Existent Creator.

The second are the properties they possess in essence, such as their brilliance and sparkle, their cleanliness and freedom from dirt and impurity and their orbital motion, whether on their own, or another, axis.

The third are the properties they possess in relation to the Necessarily Existent Being, such as their constant and undistracted witness to Him, their aspiration towards Him, their activation by His wisdom, their subservience to the perfection of His will and their movement only within His grasp, as He wishes.

He set himself to identify with each of these, to the best of his ability.

He identified with the first type by committing himself, whenever he possibly could, to the relief of any plant or animal he saw in danger, need, distress or impeded in any way. For example, if he came across a plant in permanent shadow, or one threatened by a parasite or close to death through lack of water, he would remove the obstruction if he could, separate the parasite from the host (taking care not to damage the former) or water the thirsty plant. If he saw an animal attacked by a beast of prey, caught in a snare, with a thorn in its foot, with something in its eyes or ears or suffering from hunger or thirst, he would do his best to relieve, feed or water the creature. If a riverbank collapsed or a landslide blocked a stream, denying access to animals or plants, he would clear the obstruction. He applied himself thoroughly to this type of identification.

In pursuit of the second type, he kept himself clean at all times, washing as often as possible to remove the dirt and the grime from his body. He cleaned his teeth and nails and washed his armpits and groin. He perfumed himself as he could with plant fragrances and aromatic oils and kept his clothes clean and scented, until he quite sparkled with cleanliness, fragrance, smart grooming and good looks. He also took up various kinds of orbital movement. He walked around the island's coast-line, turned circles on the shore and spun in secluded places. He made circuits around his house or a small hill, at running speed or walking and, sometimes, spun around on the spot until he dropped down in a faint.

In pursuit of the third type, he concentrated his thoughts upon the Necessarily Existent Being and cut himself off from the attachments of the senses. He closed his eyes and blocked his ears, made a great effort not to let his imagination distract him and did his best to think only of the Necessarily Existent Being alone and associated with nothing. To promote this, he would spin around faster and faster, until his sensory perceptions gradually disappeared, his imagination and other faculties that need bodily instruments weakened and the working of his self – which is independent of the body – intensified.

There were times when his mind cleared itself of corruption and he bore witness to the Necessarily Existent Being but bodily forces would soon return to spoil it, reducing him to the lowest of the low and back once again to his previous state. If he became too weak to continue, he would have something to eat, under the conditions detailed above, then recommence his three-fold identification with the celestial bodies and persevere, struggling all the time against bodily impulses. As he achieved mastery over them, so did they fight back. But at those times when he did gain control and his mind freed itself from contamination, he received some intimation of the state of those who had reached the third stage of self-identification. This he now began to strive for by meditating on the attributes of the Necessarily Existent Being.

In the course of his intellectual speculation prior to taking up this discipline, the attributes of the Necessarily Existent Being appeared to be of two kinds: either positive, like knowledge, power and wisdom, or negative, like freedom from corporeity, its attachments and whatever is related to it, however remotely. If non-corporeity is implicit in the positive attributes whereby they contain nothing of the attributes of bodies, from which multiplicity proceeds, then neither will the Divine Essence contain a multiplicity of positive attributes. They must all derive from one concept, which is the fact of the Divine Essence. He considered how to identify himself with both kinds of attribute.

Having established that the positive attributes derive from the fact of the Divine Essence, in which there is absolutely no multiplicity (since multiplicity is one of the attributes of bodies) and that his knowledge of the Divine Essence is not a concept additional to the Divine Essence but, rather, the Divine Essence is his very knowledge of the Divine Essence, and his knowledge of the Divine Essence is itself the Divine Essence, he realised that, if it is possible for him to know the Divine Essence then his knowing the Divine Essence would not be a concept additional to the Divine Essence but would be He Himself. He thus understood that his identification with Him in respect of the positive attributes should be to know Him alone, without the association of any corporeal attributes. This he set himself to do.

The negative attributes all relate to freedom from corporeity, so he began removing the qualities of corporeity from himself. He had already discarded many in the course of the discipline from the previous stage, directed at self-identification with the celestial bodies, but there were still many remnants, like the spinning (movement being one of the most specifically corporeal attributes), the concern and compassion for animals and plants, and relief of their distress. All of these are aspects of corporeal attributes since such things would not be seen in the first place without a faculty that is bodily; and, of course, the labour of looking after them also involves physical effort. As they are all inappropriate to the state to which he now aspired, he began to rid himself of these qualities.

He confined himself to sitting motionless in his cave, with bowed head and lowered gaze, avoiding all perception and bodily impulse, focusing his mind on the Necessarily Existent Being alone, without association. He did his utmost to expel anything that crept into his imagination. He disciplined himself and maintained his discipline for so long that for days on end he neither ate nor moved. When he was immersed in the witness of the One, True, Necessarily Existent Being, it sometimes happened that all essences disappeared from his memory and thought except his own, essential self. Even at the times of his most intense efforts, his own self did not disappear. This troubled him because he realised it was a contamination of absolute witness and a form of association. He persisted in trying to pass from his self and clarify his witness to the Truth.

And then it came upon him. The heavens and the earth and everything in between, all spiritual forms, all corporeal powers and all forces transcendent of matter – the essences with knowledge of Being – disappeared from his mind. His own self, too, disappeared with them. Everything faded away and vanished like dust in the wind. Only the One Reality, the Eternally Existent Being, remained. And in speech that is not a concept above His Divine Essence, He asks, *To whom belongs dominion now? To God, the One, the Almighty*.[41] That he knew no speech did not prevent him understanding His words and hearing His call. He drowned in that state and there witnessed what no eye has seen, no ear has heard and no heart of man has ever felt.[42]

So do not set your heart on getting a description of what no heart has ever felt! How can something that there is no way for the heart to feel, something not of its world or its competence be described? By "heart", I do not mean the physical organ or the spirit within but the form of the spirit whose power radiates within a man's body. However, although the word can be applied to all three, there is no way for any of them to know that state and only what has been known can be expressed. To want a description is to wish for the impossible, like wanting to taste colours and asking for black to be bitter or sweet. However, I will not leave you without some indication of the wonders he witnessed at that station[43] but only by way of allegory, not by seeking to unlock the door of truth. The only way to know is to go there yourself.

So lend your heart's hearing and turn your mind's eye to what I say and perhaps you will find something to guide you on the way. However, I make it a condition that you ask me to say no more than what I put down on these pages. The scope for expression is extremely limited and trying to use words to define something which, by its very nature, cannot be expressed is a hazardous business.

He slipped away[44] from his own self and all essences and saw in being only the One, the Eternal and bore witness to the vision. When he awoke from that state of quasi-intoxication, he returned to see everything differently and now realised that he had no self to distinguish him from the Divine Essence. The truth of his self is the Divine Essence and the thing which he had once thought of as himself and distinct from the Divine Essence is nothing, in reality, but the Divine Essence.

This might be likened to sunlight becoming visible as it falls upon coarse objects. The light may be attributed to the body on which it is visible but is nothing, in reality, but the sunlight. If the object disappears, it will no longer be illuminated but the sunlight remains the same, neither diminished nor enhanced by the absence or the presence of the object. A light-receptive body will receive light but if there is no such body, there is no receptivity and no concept of receptivity.

This perception was confirmed by his knowledge that the Divine Essence is in no way multiple and that his consciousness of the Divine Essence is the Divine Essence itself. It follows that acquiring consciousness of the Divine Essence implies acquiring the Divine Essence. He had acquired that consciousness and had, therefore, acquired the Essence. The Divine Essence is only realised by itself and the very realisation is itself the Divine Essence. Therefore, he is the Divine Essence itself.

Such is the case with all transcendent essences that are conscious of the Divine Essence. He had once believed them to be many but now knew that they are one. His misapprehension had arisen from a residual, corporeal obscurity and the muddiness of sensory perceptions and would have become set in his mind had not God, in His mercy, come to his aid and guided him. Many and few, one and oneness, conjunction, wholeness and separation are all attributes of bodies and the transcendent essences with consciousness of the Divine Essence – His are the power and the glory – because they are transcendent of matter, cannot be said to be either many or one. "Many" refers to the difference between essences, while oneness only makes sense in relation to conjunction, none of which is comprehensible without compound concepts involving matter. In this context, language is very restrictive. If you talk about such transcendent essences using the plural form of ordinary language, it gives the impression that they are multiple, although they are devoid of multiplicity, while using the singular gives the impression they are one, which is impossible. I can imagine discussing this topic with a bat, its eyes hurt by sunlight that squeaks as it flutters in a circle of frenzy:

"You've got so carried away with subtlety that you've lost the instinctive common sense of rational men and abandoned the discipline of reason! Reason dictates that a thing be either one or many!"

Well, let him calm down and curb his frantic tongue. Let him exercise some self-doubt and consider the base world of the senses of which he is so much a part, in the way that Hayy ibn Yaqzan did. By one line of reasoning, Hayy saw existence as a boundless multiplicity while by another, he saw it as one and he remained unable to decide either way.

The material world gives rise to singular and plural, conjunction and disjunction, unity and separation, similarity and difference and the meanings of these words relate to the material world. So what is he to make of the divine world, of which the words "all" or "one" cannot be used and which cannot be spoken of in ordinary language without giving a false impression of its truth? Only someone who has witnessed it can know and testify to its truth.

As regards the comment: "You've got so carried away with subtlety that you've lost the instinctive common sense of rational men and abandoned the discipline of reason. Reason dictates that a thing be either one or many," well, I concede and leave him to his rational men and reason. All that he and his like mean by "reason" is the logical faculty which works upon individual objects of sensory perception and excludes consideration of the whole. The "rational men" he talks about are those who adopt this approach, to which the manner of our discourse is far superior. So he who knows only of sensory perceptions and their universals, let him close his ears and return to his clique who *know the surface of the lower life but attend not to the hereafter.*[45]

However, if you are sympathetic to this sort of allusion to what the divine world holds and do not take my words in their ordinary, literal sense, I will tell you something more about Hayy ibn Yaqzan's witness at the station of truth.

When he reached the state of total absorption, complete extinction of self and the reality of union, he bore witness to the supreme celestial sphere, with no substance beyond it, and saw an essence devoid of matter. This was neither the Divine Essence, nor the sphere itself and yet was nothing other. It was as the image of the sun reflected in a mirror, that is neither the sun nor the mirror and yet is nothing other. He saw the transcendent essence of the sphere, too beautiful and perfect and good to be described in words, too subtle to be cloaked in letters and sounds and he gazed at the utter joy and delight, ecstasy and rapture of its witness to the Divine Essence – His are the power and the glory!

He then bore witness to the essence of the next sphere – the sphere of the fixed stars – transcendent, too, of matter. It was not the Divine Essence or the essence of the transcendent, supreme sphere or the sphere itself, and yet was nothing other. It was as if the reflected image of the sun was reflected in a second mirror and, as with the supreme sphere, he saw the joy, the rapture and the ecstasy of this essence.

He bore witness to the transcendent essence of the next sphere – the sphere of Saturn – which was not of the preceding essences and yet was nothing other. It was as if the same image of the sun was reflected in yet another mirror and, as with those before, he saw the rapture and the wonder of its essence.

He bore witness to the essences of all the spheres, transcendent and devoid of matter. They were not of the essences before and yet were nothing other. It was as if the image of the sun was reflected from one mirror to the next, through the ordered hierarchy of the spheres. In each essence, he saw a beauty, wonder and joy that no eye can see, no ear can hear and no heart of man can feel.

At last he came to the sublunary world of formation and decay and saw its essence devoid of matter, not of the preceding essences he had witnessed and yet nothing other. This essence had seventy thousand faces, in each face were seventy thousand mouths and in each mouth were seventy thousand tongues, all giving tireless praise and adoration to the Divine Essence of the One, the Truth. As before, he saw the wonder and perfection of this essence, in which such multiplicity is illusion, as though it was the image of the sun, reflected from the first mirror to the last, through the ordered hierarchy of the spheres, onto choppy water.

There, he saw his own transcendent, essential self which, had it not been brought into being from non-being and were it possible to divide the essence of seventy thousand faces, we would say was one of them, and were it not for its specific connection to his originated body, we would say was unoriginated.

On this plane, he saw other essences, like his own, some belonging to bodies that had once existed and passed away and others to bodies that, like his, were still in being. Were it possible to speak of them as many, they were infinitely many. Were it possible to speak of them as one, they were one. He saw the infinite goodness, beauty and rapture of his essence and those others, which no eye can see, no ear can hear and no heart of man can ever feel. Those who would describe it cannot. Only those who have united and who know can ever comprehend.

But he saw, too, many transcendent essences, like fouled and rusty mirrors circling those bright, shining ones on which the sun's image fell but turning their faces away. He saw a ghastliness and inferiority in them that he had never thought was possible. They writhed in unrelieved torment and anguish, smothered by a vortex of agony, scorched by the fire of exclusion and split, like light in a prism, between dread and attraction.[46]

He saw yet more essences, other than those tortured ones, bursting into light then vanishing, taking shape and dissolving. He stared at them, transfixed, and saw something vast and terrible, a seething turmoil of enormous power, settling and convulsing, dispersing and re-forming. But he gazed for just a short while before his senses returned, he awoke from his quasi-intoxicated state and stumbled back from that place into consciousness. The divine world vanished and the world of the senses appeared, since it is impossible for the two to co-exist. These two worlds are like a man's two wives – if one is satisfied, the other is enraged!

Now, let's suppose you said,

"From what you have said about this vision, it would appear that, if transcendent essences pertain to a permanently existing body that does not decay, like the celestial spheres, they will exist permanently but if they pertain to a body that tends towards decay, like man, they will decay and vanish into nothing. In your example of the mirrors, the image is only as permanent as the mirror and, if the mirror decays, it follows that the image will decay and vanish, too."

I would reply,

"How quick you are to forget an agreement and to break a promise!   Did I not say that the scope for expression is limited and that, in any case, words create a false impression? You have made the mistake of assuming that the representation and the thing represented are one and the same in all   respects.   That would not be acceptable in an ordinary discussion, so why do you countenance it here?

The sun and sunlight, their form and shape, the mirrors and the images which appear in them   – none of these are transcendent of corporeity and none has any existence except with and in bodies. Their existence depends upon the body and they cease to exist when the body does.   But divine essences and sovereign spirits, being totally devoid of corporeity and its attachments, are all independent of the body. They are not bound or connected to corporeity and the presence or absence, existence or non-existence of bodies is irrelevant. They connect and bind exclusively with the Divine Essence of the One, the Truth, the Necessarily Existent Being, who is their beginning, font and cause. Their existence derives from Him; it is He who gives them permanence, eternality and sempiternality.   They have no need of bodies, rather it is bodies who have need of them. Were their non-being possible, bodies would not exist, since bodies have their source in them.   Likewise, were the non-being of the Divine Essence possible (and may His sublimity transcend the thought, there is no god but He!) then all these essences would cease to be, as would all bodies and the entire physical world. There would be nothing, since everything is interconnected.

The physical world, dependent upon the divine world, resembles its shadow but the divine world is independent of the physical world and has no need of it.   Nevertheless, it is impossible to suppose the non-existence of the physical world since, being necessarily dependent upon the divine world, its decay can only involve change, not its absolute non-being.   This is the meaning of the Glorious Book when it speaks of mountains trembling and becoming balls of wool, of people becoming moths, of the rolling up of the sun and moon and the boiling of the sea *on a day when earth and the heavens are changed into something other than they are.*[47]

It is this power which has made it possible for me to give you some idea of what Hayy ibn Yaqzan witnessed at the sublime station. But ask me to describe no more since that would be asking for the impossible. Now, God willing, I will finish the story for you.

When he returned to the physical world after his journey, its burdens lay heavy upon him and he longed deeply for the higher life. He began the quest to return to that place in the same way as before but this time he found it easier and was able to remain there longer. And when he rejoined the world of the senses afterwards, he took up the quest again, finding it easier to reach and to maintain than the first or second times. Each time it became easier to engage with the sublime station and to remain there longer, until he was able to engage and disengage himself at will. He stayed there constantly, leaving only on account of his bodily needs which had, anyway, been reduced to the absolute minimum. He longed, above all, for God to release him from the body which demanded that he disengage from the station, and so devote himself constantly to its rapture and be free from the distress he felt whenever he was obliged to leave it to attend to physical necessity.

So he remained until he had passed the seventh septenary of his life – *i.e.* the age of fifty – at which point he happened to make the acquaintance of Absal. God willing, I will now tell their story.

*

One of the two versions of Hayy ibn Yaqzan's origins mentioned the existence of a neighbouring island and to that island a true faith based upon the teachings of one of the ancient prophets (may God bless them), had come. This religion represented truths by sketching vague outlines in the mind through the use of parables and allegory, as is usual in addressing the masses. It spread steadily throughout the island and flourished to the point where it was adopted by the king who, henceforth, imposed its observance upon the people.

Two sons of the island, young men of good-will and honour by the names of Absal and Salaman, encountered this faith and embraced it wholeheartedly. Together, they committed themselves to following its teachings and upholding its duties and rituals.

Together, they studied those parts of scripture which described God and His angels, and punishment and reward in the hereafter. Absal was interested in esoteric interpretation and spiritual meaning, while his friend Salaman was concerned with literal meaning and had little time for interpretation, contemplation and independent judgement.[48] Nevertheless, each applied himself to doing good works, examining conscience and controlling desire.

Certain passages of scripture encouraged retreat from the world and solitary meditation, indicating that therein lay salvation and success, while others advocated social engagement and commitment. His contemplative nature, desire for understanding and eagerness for insight into deeper meaning led Absal to advocate the pursuit of solitude and he drew support from verses recommending this. The solitary life, he believed, was the path to the achievement of his aim. Salaman, averse to contemplation and personal choice, urged commitment to society and similarly referred to appropriate passages of scripture for support. Commitment, he believed, was what kept the whisperings of negative thoughts at bay and protected against the temptations of demons.

Their difference of opinion led to the two parting company. Absal knew of the neighbouring island (the one where Hayy ibn Yaqzan was living), its resources, abundance and temperate climate and that solitude was there for whomever so sought it. Deciding to withdraw from society and spend the rest of his life there, he collected what money he had, spent some on the hire of a boat and divided the rest among the poor. He bade farewell to his friend Salaman and set off across the sea. The ship's crew ferried him to the island, set him ashore and sailed away.

Absal stayed on the island to worship and glorify God and contemplate His names and sublime attributes. There was nothing to disturb his mind or cloud his meditation. As need arose, he picked fruit or hunted to satisfy his hunger and, for a time, remained in perfect happiness and communion with his Lord. Daily, he witnessed His goodness, benevolence and grace towards him in easing his quest and sustenance. This gladdened his heart and confirmed his certainty.

Hayy ibn Yaqzan, meanwhile, was totally absorbed at the stations of sublimity. He only left his cave once a week to search for the food he needed. Consequently, Absal did not come across him at first and, although he wandered the length and breadth of the island, he saw no sign of anyone. This increased his sense of communion and joy, since it was the pursuit of solitude that had led him to renounce society. One day, however, it happened that Absal was in the area when Hayy emerged to look for food and they caught sight of one another.

Certain that here was a solitary ascetic, come to the island to withdraw from society as he had himself had done, Absal was afraid to intrude and make Hayy's acquaintance lest he disturb his state of mind and frustrate the fulfilment of his aim. For his part, Hayy had no idea who or what Absal was, never having set eyes on any animal like him before. He was wearing a kind of loose black tunic made of hair and wool that Hayy thought was his skin. He stood staring at him for a long time, astonished.

Afraid of disturbing him, Absal retreated. Natural inquisitiveness, however, made Hayy follow but, seeing how anxious the other was to avoid him, he kept his distance and himself, out of sight. Believing that Hayy had left the area, Absal began to pray, recite scripture, invoke God's names and prostrate himself in humility in order to calm his mind. Unnoticed to Absal, however, Hayy had crept up close enough to see and hear him in his devotions. He listened to the lovely, rhythmical sound of his voice intoning scripture and watched him humble himself in prayer, something which he had never known any other animal do. He studied his shape and appearance and realised they were the same as his own; and it was obvious that the tunic he wore was not his natural skin but something made, like his.

Appreciating that Absal's prayer, humility and devotion was something good, he became convinced he was an essence that is conscious of the Truth. He wanted to find out what he was up to and what the reason was for his prayer and devotion. He drew closer until, suddenly, Absal became aware of his presence and fled. Hayy gave chase and, with his natural strength and cunning, caught up with Absal and pinned him firmly to the ground.

Absal stared at this man dressed in furs, whose hair had grown so long that most of it reached the ground. He realised that Hayy's speed and physical strength were much greater than his own and tried to appease and placate him in a language that Hayy could not understand – he knew only that it betrayed all the signs of fear. Hayy tried to calm Absal with sounds he had learned from the animals and by patting his head. He stroked his cheeks and smiled at him until, eventually, Absal regained composure and realised that Hayy meant him no harm.

Absal's devotion to scriptural interpretation had led him to learn many languages fluently and he began to ask Hayy questions in every language he knew in an effort to make himself understood but to no avail. Hayy was puzzled by what he heard but had no idea what it meant, except that it seemed to be friendly. Each thought the other so very strange.

Now, Absal still had left a little of the food which he had brought from his own island and he offered this to Hayy. Never having seen anything like it before, Hayy did not know what it was. Absal ate a little and gestured for Hayy to eat as well. Conscious of his dietary rules, Hayy was uncertain whether or not he should accept the offer and, not knowing what it was, refused. However, Absal insisted and was behaving so kindly towards him that Hayy did not want to give offence by continuing to refuse and so he finally accepted. Having tasted and enjoyed the food, he then felt bad about what he had done and regretted breaking his own rules. He wanted to get away and devote himself to the return to his sublime station, although it would not be easy. Still, he thought that by remaining with Absal in the material world until he had found out all about him and no longer felt any curiosity towards him, he would then be able to return to his station without distraction. So he decided to stay.

When he discovered that Hayy could not speak, Absal stopped worrying about his faith and resolved to teach him language and instruct him in religious knowledge and practice. Thus would his reward from God be greater. Slowly at first, Absal taught him to speak by pointing at an object and pronouncing its name, repeating it and then having Hayy say the word while pointing at the thing. In this way, he gradually built up his vocabulary until, within a relatively short time, he could speak.

Absal asked Hayy about himself and how he had come to the island. Hayy replied that he knew nothing about his origin and parents, apart from the gazelle who had raised him. He described everything he could about himself and how he had advanced in knowledge and understanding until finally reaching the level of union. He described the truths and the essences, transcendent of the material world, which are conscious of the Divine Essence. He described the Divine Essence, with His attributes of goodness and as much as he could of the rapture of those who had united and the torment of those excluded, he had witnessed when he attained union.

As he listened, Absal had no doubt that everything in scripture about God, His angels, revelation, the prophets, the last day and heaven and hell was an allegory of the things which Hayy ibn Yaqzan had actually witnessed. The perception of his heart was opened, the fire of his mind was lit and he grasped the conformity between rational understanding and received wisdom. The different paths of scriptural interpretation were reconciled and all the difficulties he had encountered with scripture were resolved. What had before been ambiguous and obscure now became clear and he became a man of understanding. He looked at Hayy ibn Yaqzan with reverence and respect, realising him to be one of those close to God *who have no fear, neither do they grieve.* He undertook to serve and to follow him and be guided by him over any apparent contradictions in the teachings of his faith.

Absal told Hayy all about himself and, in answer to his questions, described conditions on his island, the level of knowledge, how the people had lived before the arrival of religion and the way that they lived now. He told him how scripture described the divine world, heaven, hell, resurrection, judgement and the true path. Hayy understood it all and saw nothing to contradict what he witnessed at the sublime station. He realised that whoever had so described and communicated it, had done so truthfully and was sincere in his claim to be a messenger of God's word. So he declared his belief and testified to the message.

Hayy asked what scripture said about religious duties and the practices of worship. Absal told him about prayer, taxation, the pilgrimage, fasting and other similar, external aspects of the faith. Hayy accepted and undertook to perform these, in line with his belief in the prophet's authenticity. There were, however, two points which surprised him and the wisdom of which eluded him.

First of all, why did this apostle use allegory in most of his descriptions of the divine world and avoid direct disclosure?[49] In consequence, people attribute a great deal of corporeity to the divine world and believe things about the Divine Essence of which it is completely devoid. He had similar misgivings about punishment and reward in the hereafter.

Secondly, why did he circumscribe religious obligations and the duties of worship yet make the acquisition of wealth and excessive consumption permissible? The result is that people occupy themselves in futile ways and turn their backs on truth. He, of course, thought that no-one need eat anything unless it was to keep body and soul together and the concept of money had no meaning for him. He found the regulations of religious law about money, such as the various aspects of taxation, buying and selling, interest and fines all very strange and long-winded.

"If people really understood," he said, "they would avoid these futile things, dispense with them entirely and devote themselves to the truth. No-one needs to be so obsessed with money and property that it has to be begged for, that hands be cut off for stealing or that lives be lost in robbery."

But he had made the mistake of assuming that people are thoughtful, perceptive and resolute. He had no idea of their stupidity, inadequacy, lack of judgement and weak character, of how *they are like cattle, but more lost.*[50]

Hayy developed a deep compassion for humanity and desire to be the cause of mankind's salvation. He became determined to go and explain the truth, in order to enlighten them. He discussed this with Absal and wondered if he could see any way of reaching his island. Absal told him about the people's lack of character and how they had turned from God's will without realising. However, as Hayy remained so attached to his idea, Absal offered encouragement, cherishing the hope that, through him, God might guide an aspiring group of friends who were closer to salvation than the rest. The two decided that, if they remained on the shore day and night, perhaps God would provide them with a way of making the crossing. This they resolved to do and offered prayers to Him for guidance.

By the grace of God, a ship that had been blown off course by the wind and waves was driven within sight of the shore. As it sailed close to land, the crew saw the two men standing on the shore and altered course. They agreed to Absal's request to take Hayy and himself aboard and a fair wind carried the ship to the island in no time at all.

The two disembarked and made their way into the city, where Absal's friends flocked to meet him. He introduced them to Hayy ibn Yaqzan, whom they greeted enthusiastically and treated with much respect and deference.   Absal advised Hayy that this was the group closest to understanding and wisdom among the entire population and that, if he was unable to teach them, he would have even less success in instructing the masses.   The island was now governed by Absal's old friend, Salaman, who believed in engagement with society and had argued in favour of outlawing asceticism.

Hayy began to teach and spread the secrets of his wisdom but had progressed only a little beyond the surface forms of things by describing what others had already given them to understand before they started to shut themselves off and shrink from what he had to say. In their hearts they resented him, even if they behaved towards him with courtesy out of consideration for a stranger and proper respect for their old friend, Absal.

Day and night, in public and in private, Hayy tried to win them over and convince them but this only increased their disdain and aversion. They wanted what was good and genuinely desired the truth but, because of their weakness of character, they were not prepared to accept what he said or follow his example by searching for the truth in the way that he had.   In fact, they only wanted to learn of the truth by conventional methods.   His hopes dashed by their reluctance, he despaired of their reformation.

Hayy then considered the different classes of society and found *each group satisfied with what it had.* They had taken their desires for idols and *their god was their passions.* Desperate to amass the dross of this world, *they are diverted by what they can accumulate, until they reach the grave.*   No counsel will avail nor good advice prevail and discussion only serves to entrench them. They have no path to wisdom and no share therein.   They are soaked through with ignorance. *What dominates their hearts is the profit they can make. God has laid a veil across their hearts, their ears and eyes and a terrible torment awaits them.*

He knew that a vortex of torment had engulfed them and the darkness of exclusion had descended. All of them, with few exceptions, adhered only to the worldly aspect of their faith. *They have thrown away and sold for a trivial price the good they did, thinking it worthless and slight.* Business and commerce have distracted them from the word of God and *they fear not a day when hearts and minds will be turned upside down.*

Realising this, it became perfectly clear that speaking to people of the path of illumination was impossible and it was asking too much of them to do any more than they already did. Scripture is only of any benefit to the great mass of people as it deals with the material world, to establish the proper framework and bounds of social behaviour. Only the rare exception, *the believer who strives for and devotes himself to the tilth of the hereafter*, will find the happiness of the divine world. *The dwelling of the man who wrongs others and follows the way of the lower life shall be the inferno of hell.*

What is more awful or miserable than the man who, when what he has done from the time he wakes until the time he goes to bed is examined, is seen to have done nothing but spend his day in pursuit of as many sordid sensations as he can, be it amassing wealth, procuring pleasure, gratifying lust, giving vent to rage, winning status, flaunting his piety or saving his own skin? *These are all squalid vices, one on top of another, in a fathomless sea. That there is not one of you who shall not enter hell, is God's absolute decree.*

Now aware of the people's condition and how the majority are just like dumb animals, he understood that it is impossible for all the wisdom, guidance and success of which the prophets spoke and which is contained in scripture, to be any more than it is. There are men for every task and everything is made easy for its purpose. *Thus has God dealt with those who passed before you and there is no change to how He deals.*

So Hayy went to Salaman and his colleagues, apologised for what he had spoken of and retracted it. He told them that he now took their view and would, henceforth, be guided by their example. He advised them to remain within the guidelines of scripture and ritual and not become involved with what does not concern them. He urged them to have faith in and accept the obscure passages of scripture, to uphold tradition and avoid innovation and heresy. He was particularly careful to warn them not to neglect the articles of faith or abandon themselves entirely to worldly matters, as the masses had done.

He and his friend Absal realised that this little group, aspiring but of limited ability, would only succeed by taking that road. Trying to go beyond, to the plateau of vision and perception, would only disturb and upset them and make it impossible for them to be truly happy. They would waiver and lose their grip, with unfortunate consequences. But by continuing on their present course for the remainder of their lives, they would, in the end, achieve peace and be among those who sit at God's right side.

As for *those who came first for they are the closest to God*, they bade farewell to the group and slipped back to their island to which, by God's grace, they had a safe and easy passage. Hayy ibn Yaqzan set out for his sublime station in the same way as before and found his way back. Absal followed his guidance to the point where he came close to him. And the two of them worshipped God there, on the island, until life's one certainty came to them.

***

This (and may the Spirit of God aid us both) has been the story of Hayy ibn Yaqzan, Absal and Salaman. It has discussed issues not found in books or heard in conventional discourse. It has dealt with a hidden knowledge that those who know God will accept and the deluded will simply ignore.

I have diverged from the traditional line by not withholding this knowledge. In fact, I have been prompted to draw aside the veil from this secret by the appearance in our times of insidious ideas dredged up and spread about by would-be philosophers.[51] These ideas have pervaded the country and caused widespread mischief. People imagine them to be esoteric ideas withheld from all but the elect and this has increased their interest and appetite for them. I fear for weak-minded folk who, in trying to imitate these ignorant clowns, have discarded the traditional faith of the prophets. It is my belief that, by showing folk a glimpse of the secret of secrets, they can be diverted from that trail and led towards critical examination. However, I have not left the secrets set down in these few pages without the covering of a thin veil – a veil that will be drawn aside with ease by the deserving but remain impenetrably dense to the unworthy.

I ask those of my colleagues who might read this narrative to accept my apologies for its over-simplification and loose argument. I elected to take this approach because, although the eye cannot focus on the heights I have scaled, I wished to give some approximation in language in order to awaken and quicken the desire to set out upon the path.

I ask God in His bountiful grace for His pardon and forgiveness. May He lead me to drink at the well of His serene wisdom. And upon you,

65

dear friend, whom it is my duty to assist, may there be the peace, the compassion and the blessings of God.

NOTES

[1]Abu 'Ali Hussayn ibn Sina' (Avicenna), 980-1037 – the Sheikh and Master – is one of the most original and respected philosophers of Islam. Born at Afshana, in present-day Iran, educated in Bukhara and by profession a physician, he later became political counsellor and his writings reflect his practical experience in these fields. For Avicenna, the human perfection lay in both knowledge and action. Occupied with professional duties by day, he spent his nights writing and holding seminars with students. It appears these were often lively affairs, accompanied by musical and other diversions. The extant corpus of his writings is considerable, much of it written under extremely adverse conditions, in prison or in hiding. He made contributions to all the known sciences of his day but it is for his contributions to medicine and philosophy that he is best known. The monumental *Canon Avicennae* is one of the most influential books in the history of medicine and served as the basis for seven centuries of teaching and practice, maintaining its authority in European universities until the early seventeenth century. His other major work, *The Healing*, is an encyclopaedia of philosophy and science. Many of Avicenna's writings were translated into Latin and their arguments informed the work of Christian scholastics from Bacon to Ockham. See *Encyclopaedia of Islam*[2], Vol. III, *s.v. Ibn Sinâ'* (A.-M. Goichon) and L. E. Goodman, *Avicenna* (London, Routledge: 1992).

[2]Attributed to the Persian Sufi Abu Yazid Boustami (died *circa* 875).

[3]Attributed to Hussayn ibn Mansour Hallaj, whose execution in 922 for making such theopathic remarks ("enthusiastick notions" as Ockley describes them) was a salutary experience for the Sufis; see *Encyclopaedia of Islam*[2], Vol. III, *s.v. Hallâdj* (L. Massignon / L. Gardet).

[4]This line by the poet Ibn Mu'tazz (861-908) appears in Ghazzali's spiritual autobiography, *The Deliverance from Error*.

[5]Abu Bakr Muhammad ibn Sa'igh, known as Ibn Bajja (Avempace), was born in Saragossa around the end of the eleventh century, later living in Seville, Granada and Oran; he died in Fez, in 1139, apparently poisoned. He was a philosopher, poet and musician who lived an eventful and politically active life but, lacking Ibn Tufayl's patronage, spent much of it in prison for giving expression to views out of line with the religious intolerance rife under the Almoravid rulers of Andalusia (the writings of Ghazzali were publicly burned at this time). Although not the first Andalusian philosopher – the much persecuted hermit of the Cordovan mountains, Ibn Masarra, preceded him by a century – he is held to be the first of real merit. Ibn Bajja's philosophy is characterised by a renewed

interest in Aristotle – cf. his *On the Soul*. He wrote extensively on botany and much of the natural philosophy in *Hayy ibn Yaqzan*, it may be noticed, is Aristotelian.   Ibn Bajja extended Farabi's political thought but, perhaps given his own experience of persecution, his writing betrays disillusionment with society, which he sees as materialist and corrupt.   The true philosopher – who will always live a life of estrangement – must rise above this corruption and he envisages such a man emigrating to live a life of solitary reflection within the least imperfect of imperfect societies. Their is an echo of this social pessimism in the last section of *Hayy ibn Yaqzan*.   See *Encyclopaedia of Islam*[(2)], Vol. III, *s.v. Ibn Bâdjdja* (D. M. Dunlop).

[6]Ibn Bajja, *risâlat fî-ittisâl al-'aql bi'l-insân* [Treatise on the Conjunction of the Intellect with Man], ed. M. Asin Palacios, Al-Andalus, Vol. 7, 1942, pp. 22-23; the tortuous original bears out Ibn Tufayl's later comment that his predecessor's style leaves something to be desired.

[7]Suhrawardi defines *sakîna*, translated here as "perfect stillness" as "one or more flashes of ecstasy, transient or lasting; a sublime state from which arise all sublime states".

[8]Avicenna's discussion of mysticism can be found in French translation; see A.-M. Goichon (trans.), *Kitâb al-ishârât wa'l-tanbîhât / Livre des directives et remarques* (Paris & Beirut, UNESCO: 1951), p. 483 ff., where Avicenna relates what has been told to him by a mystic. This work may represent a part of his *Oriental Philosophy*.

[9]French translation: A. Anawati (trans.), *La Métaphysique du Shifâ'* (Paris, Vrin: 1958)

[10]Ibn Tufayl's Spanish translator, Gonzalez-Palencia, attributes this verse to the Toledan poet Hisham ibn Ahmad Waqqashi (1017 - 1096).

[11]"still at the formative stage": this has been understood as a reference to Averroes.

[12]Abu Nasr Muhammad Farabi (Alfarabius or Avennasar) was born in Turkestan and lived most of his life in Baghdad; he died *circa* 950. As the first important commentor and interpreter of Aristotelian thought in Arabic, Farabi was profoundly influential upon the subsequent development of philosophy and logic in the Islamic world. In fact, he established the character of Islamic philosophy. The issue of just rule is discussed in *The Principled Beliefs of the Superior Community*.   As Ibn Tufayl indicates, Farabi believed human reason to be superior to religious faith. Faith provides only an approximation to the truth for non-philosophers. Its rituals and symbols are specific to individual cultures while the logically established truths of philosophy are universally valid. Much of his work is nevertheless concerned to demonstrate how the Greek philosophical tradi-

tion could address many of the issues raised in contemporary Islamic discussion. Farabi envisaged a perfect nation state where true philosophers would hold political office. See *Encyclopaedia of Islam*[2], Vol. II, *s.v. al-Farâbi* (R. Walzer).

[13]French translation: T. Sabri (trans.), *Traité des opinions des inhabitants de la cité idéale* (Paris, Vrin: 1990).

[14]Abu Hamid Muhammad Ghazzali (Algazel), 1058-1111, theologian, jurist and Sufi, was born at Tus, near Meshhed, Iran, and moved to Baghdad in 1091, where he taught for four years and acquired a very distinguished reputation. He abandoned professional life for eleven years and nothing is known for certain about him until 1106, when he appears in Nishapur. He seems to have spent the intervening period living variously in the Middle East and Levant as an itinerant Sufi. His best known work, *The Revival of the Religious Sciences*, from which the allegory of the blind man gaining the power of sight is taken, was composed at this time. He is credited with the introduction of a number of philosophical elements, particularly logical method, into Islamic theology. However, with his antagonism to metaphysics, Ghazzali branded philosophy with the stain of heterodoxy and relegated it to peripheral status within Islamic thinking. Although a Sufi, he is the closest of those discussed by Ibn Tufayl to mainstream Islamic theology and is sometimes called "the proof of Islam". Comparisons can be misleading but the extent of Ghazali's influence within Islam has been likened to that of St. Augustine and St. Thomas within Christianity.

[15]French translation: H. Hachem, *Le critère de l'action* (Paris, Maisonneuve: 1945).

[16]In *The Deliverance from Error*, Ghazzali admits to being a Sufi but does not suggest that he rejects belief in the physical resurrection; for an English translation, see W. M. Watt, *The Faith and Practice of al-Ghazzali* (London, 1963).

[17]The relevant passage, in W. H. T. Gairdner (trans.), *Al-Ghazzâli's Mishkât al-Anwâr: The Niche for Lights* (London: 1924), p. 96, is:

> These [three], then, are grades all of which are veiled by Lights without admixture of Darkness... But those who Attain make a fourth grade, to whom, in turn, it has been made clear that this Obeyed-One, if identified with Allah, would have been given attributes negative of His pure Unity and Perfection, on account of a mystery which it is not in the scope of this book to reveal; and that the relation of this Obeyed-One to THE REAL

> EXISTENCE is as the relation of the Sun to Eternal
> Light, or of the live coal to the Elemental Fire; and so
> "turned their faces" from him who moves the heavens
> and him who issued the command ... for their moving,
> and Attained with an Existent who transcends ALL that
> is comprehensible by human sight or human insight.

Ghazzali passes on without further comment. For a French translation, see R. Deladrière, *Ghazâli, Le Tabernacle de Lumières – Mishkât al-Anwâr* (Paris, Seuil: 1981), p. 94.

[18]Ibn Tufayl alludes here to the Prophet's *isrâ'*, or miraculous night journey, from Mecca to Jerusalem, mentioned in Quran XVII, 1.

[19]Although Gauthier's text has *Asal*, Avicenna used the name *Absal*.

[20]Quran L, 37.

[21]The Arab geographers divided the world into seven regions, each parallel to the equator; the fourth region included Spain, Greece, Syria, Iraq and Persia.

[22]An Andalusian folk-tale has been suggested as the source for this alternative account of the origins of Ibn Tufayl's hero and some of the subsequent narrative detail; a similar theme is found in Euripides' *Ion*. However, it does not seem to hold the author's interest (but see note 26); it is the first, doctrinally unsound, account of random conception from the churning clay upon which Ibn Tufayl dwells.

[23]The Arabic *tâbût* (here, "chest") occurs in Quran XX, 39 to refer to the cradle in which Moses was abandoned.

[24]Arabic *amshâj*, translated by Ockley as "seminal humours"; cf. M. M. Pickthall (trans.), *The Meaning of the Glorious Koran* (London, Knopf: 1930), LXXVI, 2: *We create man from a drop of thickened fluid* [*amshâj*].....

[25]Some modern research has suggested that biological evolution may have begun within layers of clay; see A. G. Cairns-Smith & H. Hartman (eds.), *Clay Minerals and the Origin of Life* (Cambridge University Press: 1986).

[26]It has been suggested that, with this remark, Ibn Tufayl endorses the second account of Hayy's origin, *i.e.* the result of a clandestine relationship; see H. Fradkin, *The Political Thought of Ibn Tufayl* in *The Political Aspects of Islamic Philosophy: Essays in Honor of Muhsin S. Mahdi*, ed. C. E. Butterworth (Harvard, Harvard University Press: 1992), pp. 234-261.

[27]cf. Aristotle's notion of the heart, not the brain, as the essential organ of life.

[28]Perhaps this is the pleural membrane.

[29]Quran V, 31 tells of how, after Cain's murder of Abel, *God sent a raven to scratch at the earth, to show him how to bury his brother's body...*

[30]Arabic *ṣûra* can be translated as "form" or "image".

[31]Literally, "extension in three dimensions".

[32]Quran VIII, 17.

[33]This ingenious piece of sophistry was employed by both Avicenna and the earlier philosopher Abu Yousuf Ya'qoub al-Kindi (died *circa* 866).

[34]the two brightest stars of Ursa Minor (β and γ).

[35]This is a factual error. The distance between Earth and the planets is variable, as is apparent by the difference in brightness and apparent size of, for example, both Mars and Venus, at certain times; this observation had been made in ancient times.

[36]This is explained (L. Gauthier: *Hayy ibn Yaqdhân*, p. 60, note) as a reference to a slow, regressive movement of the moon and planets, inverse to the diurnal movement of the sky – *i.e.* precession.

[37]Quran LXVII, 14.

[38]Quran XXXVI, 82.

[39]Quran XXXIV, 3; this is one of the verses adduced by Ghazzali to prove that the philosophers' view that God has no knowledge of particulars contradicts the explicit text of the revelation.

[40]Arabic *dhât*, in its technical sense, means "essence" but when applied to an individual seems better translated as "being" or "self". A problem arises – one that exercised many a mediaeval scholar's mind – when it is applied to God, in whom being and essence are one. This only confirms Ibn Tufayl's opinion that "words create a false impression" and my solution here is to paraphrase it as "Divine Essence".

[41]Quran XL, 16.

[42]cf. the following *ḥadîth qûdsi* (*i.e.* the word of God reported by the Prophet but not incorporated in the Quran): "I have prepared for my virtuous servants what no eye has seen, no ear has heard and no heart of man has ever felt" – Wensinck, *Concordance et Indices de la Tradition Musulmane*, Vol. 1 (Leiden, E. J. Brill: 1936), p. 47 and Vol. 4 (1962), p. 451.

[43]"Station" (*maqâm*) is defined by Suhrawardi as "the [acquired] ability to achieve a thing when desired, without mental effort, exertion or difficulty". The Sufi path to union with God involves passing through a number of consecutive stages or stations.

[44]*fanâ'* is defined by Suhrawardi as "the slipping away of the soul's perception of itself as a result of the intensity of its absorption in an essence wherein it finds rapture. When the perception of everything, including that of the slipping away itself, slips away, there is complete extinction of the self."

[45]Quran **XXX**, 7.

[46]The Arabic phrase here means "sawn apart" however, "sawn sections" (*manshûrât*) are what the Arab astronomers called "spherical prisms" and this, together with the preceding images of light, suggests the translation.

[47]Quran XIV, 48.

[48]The issue of the approach to scriptural knowledge – which has a long and contested history within Islam – will be dealt with more fully by Ibn Rushd.

[49]*mukâshafa*, "direct disclosure", is defined by Suhrawardi as "the soul's acquisition of knowledge, either by meditation, intuition or intimation"; it is also used as a synonym for *ishrâq*, "illumination" or "enlightenment".

[50]Quran VII, 179: [those destined for hell] *have hearts with which they do not understand, eyes with which they do not see and ears with which they do not hear. They are like cattle, but more lost....*

[51]I have been unable to identify what these insidious ideas were but the growth of secretive and hierarchic religious brotherhoods, possessing elaborate doctrines inspired by a *mélange* of mysticism, philosophy and astrology, was a feature of the times.